D1544503

BRINGIN' IN THE RAIN

BRINGIN' IN THE RAIN

A Woman Lawyer's Guide to Business Development

SARA HOLTZ

ClientFocus

Granite Bay, California

ISBN 978-0-9818140-3-2

Publisher's Cataloging-in-Publication Data

Holtz, Sara.
  Bringin' in the rain : a woman lawyer's guide to business
  development / Sara Holtz.
  p. cm.
  ISBN 978-0-9818140-3-2
  Includes bibliographical resources.
1. Lawyers—United States—Marketing. 2. Legal services—United States—Marketing.
3. Women lawyers—United States—Marketing. 4. Advertising—Lawyers—United States.
5. Women-owned business enterprises—Management. I. Title.

KF316.5 H65 2008
340/.068/8 21—dc22   2008932102

FIRST EDITION

ClientFocus
5320 Olive Tree Ct.
Granite Bay, CA 95746

Printed in Canada

To Pearl and Arthur Holtz and Ted and Billy Marsden—
from generation to generation

Acknowledgments

To my long-time dear friend, Pam Laird, without whom this book would never have existed. She showed me how I, a reluctant writer, could make it happen. And along the way, she provided invaluable advice and support—from thorough critiques of the various drafts to tips on how to overcome writer's block.

To all the women who have participated in ClientFocus' Women Rainmakers Roundtables. You are too numerous to mention by name, but you have all played a critical role in making this book a reality. Not only are you my clients, but so many of you have become my close friends. I have learned so much from you. You may think of me as the "teacher," but, in fact, most of what I know about business development I have learned from you—from your successes and your failures (which you have so candidly shared with me). Without your openness and intelligence, this would have been a very thin book, indeed.

To three guys who provided detailed, thoughtful comments on this book: Dave Marsden, my husband, who brought his keen marketing eye and experience to my work all these years and to this book in particular; Peter Zeughauser, my dear friend and former partner in ClientFocus, who has always been a huge supporter of my work and whose visionary perspective on the legal profession has shaped much of my thinking; Bob Latham, my client, whose writing flair I strive to emulate.

To my newsletter editor, Jessica Albon, who was the first person to suggest that my monthly columns could be more than just that, and who, for many years, has turned my lawyerly writing into more lively prose. To my book editor, Barbara McNichol, who has done the same with this book.

To the ClientFocus team—Danielle Donaldson, Lisa Towery, and Julia Stanley—without whose dedicated support I would never have had the time to write this book.

Contents

Introduction

I want you to be a rainmaker. Why? Because rainmakers:

- Make more money
- Have more interesting practices
- Gain power within their firms
- Enjoy the security that comes with a solid client base
- Have more control of their life and their careers

When you have your own book of business, you don't depend on others to ensure a steady, lucrative flow of work. You have more control over the clients with whom you work, how you work, and what matters.

What's more, with your own book of business, you can choose to stop working with those difficult clients who make "emergency" calls on Friday afternoon or reward your excellent work by sitting on your bill for months. You don't have to deal with that partner who needs an anger-management course or schedules out-of-town meetings on the day of your daughter's piano recital. And when the ax is falling in your firm, having a portable book of business provides you with security and gives you options you might otherwise not have—just ask any headhunter.

Overall, having your own book of business gives you the clout within your firm to influence what practices are expanded, what behaviors are rewarded, and what policies are implemented. With it comes respect— both from the colleagues in your firm and the community at large.

If you're an associate, most firms require that you demonstrate potential for bringing in business before you will be considered for partnership. In many firms, you must show you've already brought in new business.

WOMEN AND RAINMAKING

For too long, women have been reluctant to set being a rainmaker as a goal. Because they felt they didn't have the time, hadn't been anointed to inherit a retiring partner's book of business, or didn't have a booming voice that commanded attention, they believed they couldn't hope to develop their own books of business.

My experience working with women lawyers has taught me otherwise. This is not to say that succeeding as a rainmaker is easy for women (or men). But following the strategies in this book will help you reap the rewards of having your own book of business.

Why accept business development advice from me? I have been helping hundreds of women lawyers from leading law firms become rainmakers since 1995. My practice works exclusively with lawyers, and the majority of my clients are women partners.

Prior to becoming a business development coach, I had a lengthy, successful career as both a lawyer and client. I have been Vice President and General Counsel of Nestlé Beverage Company, Division Counsel for the Clorox Company, and the first woman Chair of the Association of Corporate Counsel. Having graduated from Harvard Law School and having served as an associate at a major law firm, I understand the world in which women in private practice work.

Most important, my approach to business development (as explained in this book) has produced dramatic results. Many clients who came to me with no book of business now have multimillion-dollar portfolios. Others have reported increases of more than 400 percent in their business. What do these successful women lawyers have in common?

- A willingness to take action and build their client base, not just rest on their laurels as accomplished legal practitioners
- A commitment to make marketing a priority, not just an activity that falls to the bottom of their to-do lists
- A clear focus on the type of clients to whom they should be marketing
- A recognition that strong, personal relationships form the core of successful business development
- An acceptance that, without consistent follow-up, few marketing efforts will pay off
- A willingness to ask for business at the appropriate time

HOW TO GET STARTED

This book is built on the concept of action—taking concrete, specific steps that can make you a rainmaker. There's a lot of information in these pages, and it's easy to feel overwhelmed by thinking that there's so much you need to do to put these strategies into play. Just keep in mind that "overwhelm" is the enemy of "action," so take your time and work in stages.

Instead of setting out to do everything in this book, commit to doing *something*. Start with what seems natural and easy for you, and just do it. I suggest operating about 10 percent outside your comfort zone to see what results you can achieve. Also commit to stop doing things that are not producing results. When you discontinue them, you free up time and energy to try out one of the new strategies from the many detailed here.

WHAT YOU'LL FIND IN THIS BOOK

Nearly 50 strategies are presented in the following nine chapters. Each one features specific Rainmaking Action Steps for you to implement immediately. Throughout the book, I include sidebars of real-life examples from my coaching practice to illustrate these strategies in action.

Chapter 1: Focus Your Marketing Efforts deals with eight business development strategies that will help you target your marketing to get the greatest payoff. You will learn how to develop a detailed vision for what you want your practice to look like and who you want your clients to be. You will find time-tested strategies for identifying your target market, enabling you to focus your energies where they are likely to produce the best results. You'll learn how to prioritize and focus your marketing efforts, and you'll discover the advantages of narrowing your practice to position you as the go-to person for particular matters.

Chapter 2: Engage in High-Payoff Activities helps you to identify the specific marketing activities that are most likely to produce results, given who you are and what your practice is. You will be encouraged to examine what has worked for you in the past and what strengths you can leverage for business generation. You will see how important it is to make existing clients a priority in your marketing mix, and you'll discover how to overcome the obstacles that are standing in the way of you getting hired.

Chapter 3: Follow-Up addresses the biggest business development mistake most lawyers make—failing to follow up consistently on marketing activities. Here you'll find a variety of ways to maintain contact with potential clients. From written correspondence to phone calls, from social invitations to office visits, you'll find a wealth of opportunities to help you stay in touch.

Chapter 4: Build Strong Relationships explains the importance of creating personal relationships with clients, prospective clients, and referral sources, and provides specific suggestions on how to accomplish this. This chapter will show you how to broaden and expand your connections with others, transforming business relationships into personal relationships.

Chapter 5: Ask for Business provides guidance on how to discover the particular services clients are interested in buying and, when appropriate, how to ask for business. You will also receive specific advice on the tricky issue of asking friends for their business, and discover how to leverage your existing relationships to help you generate business through referrals and cross-selling.

Chapter 6: Make Time to Market Your Practice highlights the importance of developing a marketing mindset, setting aside time to devote to marketing, and allocating your marketing time wisely. You'll also learn how to maintain your marketing momentum. Perhaps most important, you'll discover how to tap into the schedule-freeing power of the word "no."

Chapter 7: Create a System for Your Marketing Activities shows how to develop systems that will enable you to market more efficiently and effectively. The importance of adequate preparation is stressed. This chapter also offers ideas for how to get the greatest payoff from attending networking events and conferences, giving speeches, and writing articles. It illustrates how you can seize marketing opportunities— sometimes when you least expect them.

Chapter 8: Forge Marketing Partnerships discusses how to enlist help inside and outside your firm to keep you motivated and maximize your marketing efforts. Whether it's hiring a coach or enlisting the aid of another lawyer or other professional, you'll find that the team approach can boost your marketing impact.

Chapter 9: Some Final Thoughts encourages you to develop patience in your approach to business development and offers strategies for dealing with rejection.

The **Resources** section lists reading material that are particularly relevant for women lawyers.

HOW TO USE THIS BOOK

You can apply the concepts in this book in three different ways:

> **Read through it in its entirety.**
> Doing so gives you a broad, comprehensive view of how you can become a successful rainmaker. Don't get overwhelmed

by thinking you must implement all the strategies right away. Instead, select a few that resonate with you, and act on them. I suggest paying special attention to three key sections: Chapters 1, 2, and 3.

Read a specific chapter as you encounter a related challenge in your business development efforts.
Scan the Table of Contents for subject areas and strategies of interest. For example, if you feel scattered and want to get a clearer focus for your activities, read Chapter 1. If you want to maximize your networking efforts, read "Get the Most Out of Networking Events" in Chapter 7.

Read one strategy a week and implement its Rainmaking Action Steps.
By doing this, you will have implemented all the strategies in the book within a year and still have time for a well-deserved vacation. You can even skip a few weeks when you feel swamped with client work.

Regardless of the approach you take, be sure to implement the Rainmaking Action Steps at the end of each subchapter.

CAN MEN BENEFIT FROM THIS BOOK, TOO?

The answer is a resounding *yes*. While this book focuses on women lawyers, it is a valuable resource for male lawyers as well, and its advice is largely gender neutral.

However, I have chosen to direct the content to women lawyers for four reasons:

- The vast majority of my clients are women, and therefore most of my experience involves women lawyers.
- Studies consistently show that women receive less business development mentoring than do men. My goal is to help remedy that inequity.
- Too often, women have resigned themselves to the role of being a "service partner," believing that becoming a rainmaker lies beyond their reach. This is simply not true, and is a big reason why I wrote this book.
- Women have historically not reaped the benefits of being a successful rainmaker. It's time that they did!

Put on your raincoat, turn the page, and let's get started.

CHAPTER ONE

Focus Your Marketing Efforts

When clients first come to me, they frequently complain that they don't have anyone to market to. Believe it or not, that's usually not the case. In actuality, you probably have *too many* people who comprise your potential market.

Unless you have a very narrowly focused practice (for example, representing professional soccer players), you have more than enough people to whom to direct your marketing. Your challenge is to decide where to channel your efforts so you have the best chance of getting a return on your energies.

As an example, let's take a lawyer who practices employment law in San Francisco. Her prospective marketing targets include every company in California. (I limit it to California only because much of employment law is determined by state law. If she were a securities litigator, no such geographic limitation would be applicable.) To focus her marketing, she needs to decide:

What size company will she pursue? Presumably, very small companies won't hire her because her rates are too high. Very large companies may handle most of their employment work in-house, except for major litigation.

What geographic location will she target? Will she market to all employers of a certain size in California, or will she limit her marketing to Northern California or the San Francisco Bay Area?

What types of employment problems will she handle? Is she interested in working on all types of matters—from reviewing employee manuals to litigating wage and hour class-action litigation? Or does she focus on specific employment problems, such as sexual harassment? Perhaps she wants to specialize solely on high-exposure litigation, which is more profitable than counseling.

Will she target specific industries? Software development companies present different types of employment law issues than do manufacturing companies.

The answers to each of these questions will dramatically affect how this employment lawyer goes about her marketing efforts.

The opposite of having a clear focus for your marketing efforts is committing "random acts of lunch." For example, your roommate from law school goes in-house. She quickly becomes the center of your marketing, regardless of whether her company has a need for your services or is a good fit for your practice—or if your friend is even in a position to hire you.

Rather than being opportunistic, your challenge is to be strategic—deciding, after careful analysis, who will be on the receiving end of your marketing efforts instead of wasting time on random prospects. This is what this chapter is designed to help you do.

DEVELOP A CLEAR VISION

The first step in focusing your marketing efforts is to develop a vision for your practice. This enables you to attract the types of clients and matters that will further your professional and personal goals.

It makes no sense to pursue business development activities that won't move you closer to your vision for your practice. Still, lawyers do this all the time. Here are two examples:

- My client is a general commercial litigator who wanted a niche practice working with the financial services industry, because she (rightly) believed her marketing would be easier and she could charge higher rates. Yet her efforts centered on speaking on general litigation topics, such as how to take a deposition. Once she became clear on the need to match her marketing activities to her vision for her practice, she altered her approach. Now she speaks only on topics specifically targeted to the financial services industry.

- A bankruptcy lawyer wanted to get clients with higher billings. Nevertheless, she continued to market to clients who had historically sent her small matters. Once she clarified her vision, she devoted her marketing to clients whose bankruptcy matters would involve much higher fees.

In developing your vision for your practice, answer these questions:

What kind of work do you want to do?
Securities litigation? Mergers and acquisitions? Entertainment law? International arbitrations?

Who are your clients?
Financial institutions? Consumer products companies?
Biotech start-ups? Real estate developers? High net-worth
individuals?

Where are your clients located?
In your city? In your state? Nationally? Internationally?

Who do you work with?
Which partners? Which associates? What kind of administrative support do you have?

How much money are you making?
How large are your originations?

What's your work/life balance like?
How many hours are you billing? How many hours do you
devote to non-billables? How much do you travel in your
work? How many vacations do you take and for how long?
How do you renew your energy?

What is your role in your firm?
What leadership role, if any, do you have in the firm? What
committees are you on? To what leadership role do you
aspire?

What other issues are important to you?
What personal or professional goals are you pursuing or have
you achieved? More time with family? More time to exercise?
More involvement with your favorite charity? More time for
hobbies?

Now summarize your answers into a succinct statement of your vision. Here's an example:

I handle sophisticated products liability litigation for three major medical device manufacturers located in New England. I am supported in my work by a junior partner and a very capable associate. I originate $1 million a year and I make $400,000 a year. I work 1,900 billable hours and 400 non-billable hours. I am away from home no more than five nights a month. I exercise three times a week and volunteer in my daughter's classroom twice a month. Our family takes two one-week vacations a year. I serve on the board of a local community theater.

Rainmaking Action Steps

▶ Take the time to think about where you want your practice—and your life—to be in three years. The more detailed your picture, the more valuable it will be in focusing your business development efforts.

▶ Write down your vision in a succinct statement.

ESTABLISH YOUR ANNUAL GOALS

Once you have a clear idea of where you want to take your practice and your life in the next few years, it's time to determine what you need to do in the next year that will get you there.

When setting your annual goals, the critical first step is making sure these goals align with your long-term vision. For example, if your three-year vision is to increase your originations by 50 percent, your goal for the coming year might be to accomplish one of the following:

- Get three new clients
- Increase your billings by 15 percent
- Cultivate three new referral sources

Each of these achievements would move you closer to making your vision a reality.

Or let's say you want to transition your general commercial litigation practice into an intellectual property litigation practice. Your short-term goal might be to:

- Work on a patent matter to gain more experience in the area, which in turn will increase your credibility with potential clients.
- Gain visibility for your IP expertise among the litigation partners in your firm so they will refer these types of matters to you.

When determining your short-term goals, be sure of two things:

- Your goal will move you toward your vision.
- Your goal is specific and realistic.

Being specific means incorporating quantifiable standards—such as numbers, dollar figures, percentages, and names—into your goal. "Get more clients" is not a specific goal; "get three new clients" is. If your goal is specific, you'll be able to see if you accomplished it at the end of the year.

Here are some examples of specific goals:

- Increase originations by 15 percent
- Get $100,000 in originations from a specific client

- Get three new construction defect litigation matters
- Get one new high-visibility environmental matter
- Cultivate three new referral sources in the aviation industry
- Receive one internal referral from a specific lawyer in your firm
- Heighten your visibility among CEOs in the wine industry
- Increase your credibility for handling software disputes with mid-sized Denver-based companies
- Expand your network at a client company by developing relationships with the Vice President for Manufacturing and the Vice President for Human Resources
- Cross-sell the firm's tax department to two clients

Being realistic means the goal is achievable in terms of the time and resources you're able to invest in business development. It is important that your goals be realistic so you don't set yourself up for failure by making them too ambitious (which is a common problem for lawyers).

Rainmaking Action Steps

▶ Based on your vision, write down one or two goals on which you will focus your business development efforts in the next 12 months.

▶ Make sure your goals are specific and realistic.

▶ Make sure that achieving your goals will move you closer to your vision.

IDENTIFY YOUR IDEAL CLIENT

You simply cannot market to everyone who could use your services. So why not limit your marketing efforts to people with whom you'd love to work rather than use your precious time garnering more work from less-than-ideal clients?

Here are three benefits to defining your ideal client and directing your marketing to them:

- Your enthusiasm for marketing will increase if you think it will net clients with whom you'd really like to work.

- In all likelihood, you will do outstanding work for such clients. (We tend to do our best work for those we like the most.)

- Working for ideal clients is much less time consuming and resource draining than working with "nightmare" clients who require a disproportionate amount of your time and energy.

It may seem like a pipe dream to think you can fill your practice with "ideal" clients, but if you have a choice (and, of course, you do), it makes sense to invest your marketing time in the clients you most want to have. If you market to people who don't meet your ideal profile, you'll fill your practice with exactly those clients.

> **Here's a description of the "ideal" client provided by one of my clients:**
>
> *My ideal clients are the general counsels of healthcare systems in the Northeast, with a budget for outside counsel in the $500,000 to $1,000,000 range. The issues I am hired to work on are central to their business. They're interested in building*
>
> *continued*

> *a long-term relationship with their outside counsel. They're smart, decisive, and communicative. They have a good sense of humor. They're willing to discuss billing expectations openly. Because they are highly satisfied with my work and know that I make their matters a priority, they're willing to be an excellent referral source to potential clients for me.*

These questions will help you profile your ideal clients:

- What type of matters do they have?
- What are the typical billings for their matters?
- What industry or industries are they in?
- Where are they located? Are they across town or around the world?
- What position do they hold in their companies? Are they businesspeople or lawyers?
- How does their work help build your expertise?
- How does their work capitalize on your strengths and experience?
- Are they likely to be a continuing source of business? Are they likely to refer you to other potential ideal clients?
- What relationship do they want to have with their lawyer? Do they work collaboratively or do they give you a lot of autonomy?
- What are their personal characteristics? Appreciative? Decisive? Communicative? Lively sense of humor?
- What characteristics do you want to avoid? Demanding? Distrustful? Slow to pay? Micromanagement?

USE THE PEBBLE-IN-THE-POND APPROACH

Given the overwhelming number of possible targets for your marketing efforts, the question becomes where to begin. The answer is simple.

- Always begin your marketing efforts with your clients—either those with whom you're currently working or those you've represented in the past.

- Once you've exhausted possibilities among that group, turn to people who have referred matters to you in the past (whether inside or outside your firm).

- Then move on to people within your firm who could refer business to you but haven't so far.

- Finally, and only after you've exhausted those three groups, turn to marketing to "strangers"—people with whom you have no previous client relationship.

For most lawyers, the best source of new business is past or current clients—whether in the form of new matters for those clients or referrals from them. Statistics consistently show that 80 percent of all new business comes from existing clients. Marketing to people who know you and your work almost always trumps marketing to strangers. When you leverage relationships with existing or past clients, your marketing activities get better results and you spend less time on business development.

It's not hard to understand why existing clients are such a good source of new business. People hire people they know, like, and trust. Clients who have worked with you know what you're capable of doing. Unless something has gone wrong in previous engagements, they trust you, which is by far the hardest element of the know/like/trust trifecta to cultivate.

Compare that known-entity situation to the scenario clients face when they hire someone with whom they've never worked before. They don't really know the new lawyer's capabilities; the relationship hasn't been developed, so they don't know how easy it will be to work with her; and, most important, no real trust has yet been established.

> A real estate lawyer with whom I work wanted, in her words, "to take my practice to the next level." She had lots of big ideas (meaning time consuming and resource intensive) for how to do this. I advised her that before embarking on those activities, she had to do one thing: meet with each of the clients she had represented in the last three years and ask them either for more work or a referral. She agreed. A month later, we spoke again. When I asked her how things were going, she told me she no longer needed my services. Her plate was completely filled with work from the meetings. It doesn't always work that way—if it did, I'd be out of business—but it does demonstrate the value of marketing to your existing clients.

Once you've exhausted gaining new business from your clients, your next step is to go back to people who have referred you to others in the past and ask for more referrals. These referral sources might be people in your firm or professionals from related fields—such as accountants, investment bankers, and consultants. They present good marketing opportunities for you because they know, like, and trust you and have demonstrated a willingness to act on your behalf. (Not all the people who "should" be good referral sources for you actually prove to be. Don't waste your time trying to convert them.)

Next, focus your marketing efforts on internal referral sources in your firm who have not yet given you business. Because these people are your colleagues, they should, at the very least, have a modicum of trust in your abilities. Again, you've addressed the critical element of the know/like/trust template.

Only after you have mined all of these relationships should you turn your energies to marketing to strangers—people with whom you don't already have a professional relationship.

I call this the pebble-in-the-pond approach to marketing, because just as tossing a pebble into a pond creates increasingly larger concentric circles, your marketing operates in the same way. The innermost circle is composed of your existing clients, which is the easiest place to start marketing. You can expand your efforts to the increasingly larger circles, but only after you've fully tapped the inner circles.

Look for new business in the right places and you are much more likely to find it.

> **Rainmaking Action Steps**
> ▶ Make a list of all the clients you've worked with during the past two years. Which of them have the greatest potential for sending new business or for referring a matter to you in the next twelve months? Start your marketing activities there.
>
> *continued*

> ▶ Make a list of all the people who have referred business to you in the last two years. Include both lawyers from within your firm and others who have served as referral sources. Of these sources, which have the greatest potential for referring new business to you in the next 12 months? Market to them after your past and current clients.

DETERMINE YOUR BEST REFERRAL SOURCES

The most likely source of new business, other than existing clients, is a referral. Yet women lawyers, for the most part, don't utilize their referral relationships as well as they could.

Many people can help you grow your business by serving as referral sources. You just need to take the time to identify those who have the potential to be good referral sources, and then actively seek their referrals. Such sources can be the targets of your marketing efforts just as prospective clients are.

To begin this process of identifying who is a high-potential referral source, think about:

Who has referred business to you in the past? Obviously, they know, like, and trust you. What can you do to strengthen that relationship? Do you stay in touch with them on a regular basis? Have you acknowledged the referrals you've received from them?

Who are your favorite clients? They've experienced your work firsthand and can talk about what an excellent job you did. Have they referred business to you recently? If not, why not? Is it because you haven't asked? Is it because you haven't educated them about who would be a good referral for you?

Who do you know through your professional or community involvements? Consultants, opposing counsel, investment bankers, and people you have worked with in professional activities all fall within this category. They have seen you in action and have confidence in your abilities. Has knowing them yielded referrals? Don't assume that these people know exactly what you do (other than that you are a lawyer) or how you are trying to develop your practice. What can you do to educate them about the scope of your practice and who would make an ideal referral for you?

For whom have you recently done a favor? People you have helped in the past may feel they "owe you one." This is true regardless of whether the favor was a personal one, such as helping them find a nanny, or a professional one, such as helping them find a job.

To whom have you referred business? Have these people reciprocated? If not, why? Do they understand that you expect some sort of reciprocity?

To be sure, some referral sources are more likely than others to produce results. The best referral sources:

Know the people you're targeting as clients. For example, if you're pursuing biotech companies, your high-potential referral sources might already work with venture capitalists who specialize in biotech ventures. Or if you're targeting in-house counsel who live in Boston, your high-potential referral source might be a member of the Boston chapter of the Association of Corporate Counsel.

Believe you'll do an excellent job. This knowledge is usually acquired from having worked with you. They may have been involved with you on a legal matter in the past—as a client, opposing counsel, or expert witness. They may have worked with you in another capacity, such as serving together on the same board. Or they may have heard from someone they trust that you're worthy of their referral.

Are willing to refer. Some people are generous with their referrals; others are not. This may have nothing to do with how well they know you or how competent they think you are; some people are just more willing than others to take a risk and recommend you.

Involve a mutually beneficial relationship. It's just human nature. If people think there's something in it for them, they're more likely to make a referral. Mutuality comes in many different forms—people may believe that you will make a reciprocal referral, they may get credit within the firm for having made the referral (either in the form of increased origination credit or "good citizen" points), or they may think that the person to whom they referred you will appreciate the referral.

The following people tend to be high-potential referral sources:

- Highly satisfied clients
- People who have referred before
- People for whom you have recently done a favor
- People with whom you have a strong professional relationship

Rainmaking Action Steps

▶ Inventory your potential referral relationships:

    ▶ List the people from whom you received referrals during the past year.

continued

> ▶ List your top five clients from the past year.
>
> ▶ List the people with whom you work in community or professional activities.
>
> ▶ List the people for whom you have recently done a favor.
>
> ▶ List the people (both attorneys and non-attorneys) to whom you have referred matters in the past year.
>
> ▶ Identify which of these people have the greatest potential to refer business to you in the next twelve months.

CONCENTRATE ON HIGH-POTENTIAL NEW CLIENTS

It would be great if all you had to do was market to people who'd already sent you business. Unfortunately, it's not always that easy.

To make the most of your limited marketing time, it's important to identify those potential clients who will give you the best return on your investment of business development time. You want to focus on high-potential opportunities—those who are:

- Most likely to need your services
- Open to hiring you
- The best fit for your ideal client profile

How do you determine if someone is a high-potential opportunity? Here are several questions to ask:

Do they need your services?
A privately held company probably doesn't need your sophisticated securities expertise. If a company handles all

of its trademark work in-house, your trademark acumen is probably not a good fit.

Are they dissatisfied with their current representation?
One of the toughest sales is trying to lure satisfied clients away from their current counsel. If they're pleased with their existing relationship, why would they go through the upheaval of a change in counsel (which requires educating the new counsel about their company, their legal department, and their management style) and take a risk on an untested lawyer? Even if you think you can do a better job than their current lawyers, remember, that's not the issue. Satisfaction is in the eye of the client, not you. If a potential client's sole dissatisfaction with current counsel is the fees being charged, you'll likely find yourself defending your position against a lower-cost provider down the road. Bargain hunters are among the toughest clients with whom to maintain loyal relationships.

Are they willing to change counsel?
Even dissatisfied clients may not be eager to change counsel. If they foresee a steep (read: expensive) learning curve on a matter, they may not be willing to make a change, even if they're not delighted with their current firm.

Can you effectively market to them?
It's just not possible to market to the world. Do you have a way to reach the clients you have in mind? Do you know them or know someone who's willing to make an introduction? Cold calling is a waste of time when selling something as complicated, expensive, and intangible as legal services.

Can they make the decision to hire you or, at the very least, influence the hiring decision?
Mid-level human resource professionals are often delighted to attend seminars to keep current on emerging laws, but they're seldom the ones who actually hire lawyers. Hiring typically happens in the legal department or the executive suite.

Can these clients afford you?
Nothing is more frustrating than landing clients who can't afford your fees. Start-ups, individuals, and small companies often fall into this category.

Is there a likelihood of a continuing relationship?
Landing new clients takes a lot of time and energy. It's better to target a company that offers the possibility of a continuing source of business (or referrals) than a one-shot engagement.

Is the work a strategic fit for your practice?
Will representing these clients help build your credibility in an area you want to develop? For example, if you want to specialize in insurance coverage litigation, a probate litigation client isn't a great fit for building your practice (unless, of course, you can get someone else to handle the matter, while you get the origination credit).

Can you represent the client without creating a conflict?
As obvious as this may seem, I have clients who have invested a great deal of time cultivating potential clients, only to realize they couldn't represent them because of a business or ethical conflict of interest within their firm.

Under your firm's compensation system, will you be rewarded for netting these clients?
Compensation systems vary from firm to firm. Some reward expanding existing client relationships (as they should); others

don't. It makes little sense to invest your precious marketing time landing potential clients for whom you will not receive credit.

Would you enjoy working with these clients?
Life is too short to spend it dealing with difficult clients.

It is likely that you won't know the answers to all of these questions, so your first marketing task is to do your homework and get the answers. Some answers can be found by doing online research. Others can be uncovered by asking your colleagues within your firm. Still others can be ferreted out by tapping into your network. But for many of these questions, you'll need to go straight to the source and ask the potential client directly.

Before marketing to a prospective client, take the time to determine whether you're directing your efforts toward high-potential opportunities. This will make your marketing much more efficient and effective.

Rainmaking Action Step

▶ Answer the questions above before you invest any significant amount of time marketing to a new client. It's unlikely that any prospect will produce a "yes" for each of these questions, but the more affirmative answers you get, the more likely that prospect will prove to be a high-potential opportunity.

INVEST IN YOUR "A LIST," STAY IN TOUCH WITH YOUR "B LIST"

In his classic book, *Animal Farm,* George Orwell wrote, "All animals are equal, but some animals are more equal than others." So it is with potential clients.

Quite simply, some are worth more of your efforts than others. To get the biggest payoff for the time you invest in marketing, spend the majority of your energy on the limited number of prospects—generally no more than ten—that have the most potential for sending you business in the near term. This is your "A list." Eighty percent of your time should be spent marketing to them. For example, if you have 200 hours a year to devote to marketing, spend about 160 of those hours marketing to these people.

Typically, your "A list" includes:

- Clients (past and current)
- Past referral sources
- A select group of internal referral sources
- A limited number of high-potential prospective clients or prospective referral sources

But what about all those other people in your Rolodex or contact management system? They have the potential to send business, but they're not "A listers," so include them in your "B list." Your "B list" consists of people to whom you market, but at a lower level of intensity. Invest about 20 percent of your available marketing time on your "B list." For example, if you have 200 hours a year to spend on marketing, devote 40 hours to those on your "B list."

The challenge with marketing to your "B list" is how to do it efficiently. Let's say your "B list" is composed of 100 people. You can't invite them out to lunch one at a time, but you do want to stay in touch with them about once a quarter.

Here are some ways you might do that:

- Send an article (written by you or someone else) with a handwritten note, explaining why you thought it might be of interest.

- Invite them to a firm-sponsored seminar.

- Send a quick staying-in-touch e-mail such as "Delighted to see that your favorite football team made the playoffs" or "I found a great new restaurant in San Francisco I think you'd enjoy the next time you're there."

- Host a luncheon for eight to ten people, all of whom have something in common (e.g., all former colleagues at your firm, all mothers of preteens, all avid book readers, etc.).

- Send personalized holiday cards in December, or better yet, send cards celebrating another holiday at an off time of year, such as the Fourth of July or Valentine's Day.

- Send an e-mail containing a link to a Web site, online article, or video of interest.

Rainmaking Action Steps

▶ Identify who is on your "A list."

▶ Go through your Rolodex or Outlook address book and create your "B list."

▶ Decide how you will stay in touch with your "A list" at least once a month and with your "B list" at least once a quarter.

CREATE A NICHE PRACTICE

When I first suggest to clients that they focus their practice by creating a niche practice, they often resist. From their perspective, having a niche is a risky strategy because it limits the number of potential clients who could send them business. But the fact is that having a niche actually makes marketing easier and more efficient. Marketing is all about standing out from the crowd in a memorable way—and that's exactly what having a niche can do for you.

If the concept of creating a niche is scary to you, remember that a niche is about where you focus your marketing, not about how you spend your day. You can still handle work outside your niche that comes in over the transom or that your partners refer to you. It's just not where you concentrate your marketing efforts.

You can define your niche by focusing on:

- A specific substantive area of law: eminent domain litigation, advertising law, consumer class actions, software licensing, or outsourcing
- A particular industry segment: academic medical centers, the hospitality industry, automobile dealers, or family-owned businesses
- A specific demographic: geographic location, a company's gross revenues, or the size of its workforce
- A combination of any of the above

My son broke his arm on the last day of school (while in math class—don't ask!). I spent three hours on the phone trying to find an available orthopedic surgeon to cast it, even though my son's pediatrician told me her physician's assistant could easily handle the task. When it comes to doctors, most people want to go to a specialist, not a generalist. You wouldn't trust brain surgery to a generalist, would you?

The advantages to having a niche far outweigh the possible disadvantages. Advantages include:

You'll be perceived as an expert. Clients will assume you're an expert because of the perceived singular scope of your practice.

You actually become an expert. The more of a particular type of matter you handle, the more you know. Your experience increases clients' confidence that you're the right person for their matter. As a related benefit, it also increases *your* confidence, which translates into more effective marketing. Finally, your increased expertise is likely to generate better results for your clients. Satisfied clients are more apt to use you again or refer you to their colleagues. The circle continues.

You'll face less price sensitivity. People pay for expertise.

You'll have less competition. Generalists have to compete with both generalists and specialists. Specialists have far fewer people to compete against. Consider the difference between the number of general commercial litigators versus the number of lawyers who specialize in litigation involving long-term healthcare facilities.

Your marketing will be simpler. You're no longer marketing to the world, but rather to a defined, relevant audience. Having a niche allows you to target your efforts. You can much more easily figure out what they read, the conferences they attend, and where they network. Also, your marketing message becomes clearer because you can more easily understand the needs of your niche client. You can then tailor your marketing message accordingly.

Prospects and referral sources remember what you do. One of the greatest challenges in marketing is maintaining what advertisers call "share of mind"—being remembered as a potential provider when a need arises. When you have a niche and someone needs your type of services, your name stands out. You become the go-to person for those types of matters.

> When I was an in-house counsel, I met dozens of commercial litigators each year. Few stuck out in my mind. But when I met people who had a particular niche—for example, premises liability or water rights litigation—they were memorable to me. Your specialty creates a clear—and lasting—picture about what you do in the minds of potential clients.

How narrow should your niche be? As small as possible while still generating what you consider sufficient business. The reality is that you don't need that many good clients to have a successful book of business.

> Many years ago, I met with a successful rainmaker and asked him about his business development goal. He wanted one more large, dependable client. He had three of them already; with one more, he figured he could rest comfortably at night. He didn't need hundreds of clients to fill his practice—just four good ones.

Rainmaking Action Step
> ▶ Decide how you can refine the description of your practice to create a niche in the minds of your prospective clients.

Having done the exercises in this chapter, you now have a clear sense of the "who" of your marketing efforts. The upcoming chapters address those activities that will help make your marketing efficient and effective.

CHAPTER TWO

Engage in High-Payoff Activities

As a busy lawyer, you want your marketing to be efficient and effective—generating the best results with the least amount of effort. There's no such thing as a "good" or "bad" marketing activity. Quite simply, effective marketing produces results; ineffective marketing doesn't.

To make the most of your efforts, it's important to pinpoint those activities that take relatively little time to bring in new business for you. These are your high-payoff activities, and you'll want to engage in them on a regular basis. It's also essential to determine those activities that are time-consuming and produce few results, so you can stop doing them.

An important fact to remember when focusing on your high-payoff activities is that what gets results for one lawyer may not work for another.

What constitutes a high-payoff activity can vary from person to person and from practice to practice, so you'll need to discover the ones that work best for you. This chapter will help you determine the specific marketing efforts that will give you the best results for the time invested.

REALIZE THERE IS NO "RIGHT WAY" TO MARKET

Ask most successful rainmakers the best way to build a book of business and they will have a ready answer, but each will likely have a different answer. Some people say it's developing a strong reputation by giving speeches. Others claim it's writing articles for legal publications. Still others believe you can distinguish yourself by earning prestigious designations, such as being ranked by Chambers or being invited to join the American College of Trial Lawyers. Some people urge you to attend countless networking events and hand out your business card to everyone you meet. Some think that having lunch every day with a different potential client is the way to go.

Within most firms, there is a presumption that there is a "best" way to market—usually based on the way the firm's biggest rainmaker has built his practice (and in most cases, it is a "he"). In truth, the "right way" to develop business is the one that works for you. It depends on:

Your strengths. Some people are great writers. Others are naturally curious and easily discover what makes potential clients tick. Some love attending networking events and meeting new people. As you read this chapter, you'll find tips to help you identify your strengths.

The activities that get you the best results. Some people get their biggest payoff from staying in touch with past and current clients. Others find that asking for referrals produces a steady stream of new business.

Still others believe that a monthly newsletter makes the phone ring. Be honest with yourself as to whether the activities in which you have historically been involved are paying off. This chapter addresses a variety of activities to help you recognize the ones best suited to you.

Where you are in your career. If you're young, you may need to focus your efforts on building your reputation. Writing, speaking, and developing a niche practice may be what's needed. If you're more seasoned, perhaps the best investment of your time is in nurturing your established relationships.

The kind of practice you have. Some practices can be marketed to the person making the hiring decision. Other practices may have to rely on marketing to referral sources. For example, if you're marketing a white-collar defense practice, it's difficult to market directly to the ultimate client. After all, you can't just call someone up and say, "Given what I've been reading in *The Wall Street Journal* about your business practices, it's my guess that you'll be hearing from the SEC soon." On the other hand, if you're marketing an environmental compliance practice, it's not difficult to identify and market to environmental compliance executives who are hiring in-house lawyers to handle environmental matters.

How your potential clients like to be pursued. Some want to meet you in person; others are happy to work with you for years and never meet face-to-face. Some love to be wined and dined; others can't accept lunch invitations without picking up their share of the tab because of their company's policies. Some like to talk on the phone; others prefer e-mail. Some like to develop a personal relationship with their lawyers; others are strictly business.

I have clients who have built their books of business by:

- Publishing articles
- Regularly attending networking events
- Speaking at conferences
- Participating in bar activities

On the other hand, I have clients—highly successful rainmakers—who have done none of these things. What's critical is to figure out what generates the most positive results for you.

Keep these factors in mind as you read the sections that follow and discover your own "right way" to market. Don't be intimidated by the conventional wisdom or "shoulds" you hear from others. They may have a different client base, feel comfortable doing different things, have different strengths, or be at a different stage in their career. What's important is what works for you.

Rainmaking Action Step

▶ Bring a critical eye to which marketing activities produce results for you.

REVIEW WHAT HAS WORKED FOR YOU

A first step to discover your high-payoff activities is to review the marketing endeavors you have pursued in the past year or two—lunches hosted, articles written, conferences attended. Which ones resulted in business? Which ones took relatively little time and produced new matters? Did work come from the speech you gave to a local industry group? Were you hired after visiting a client at his or her office? Did you get an opportunity to make a presentation to a new client because of a networking event you attended? Did you get introduced to someone you think is a high-potential opportunity by asking your partner to cross-sell you? Which activities were time-consuming and failed to produce any results?

Of course, not all activities considered to be effective marketing produce immediate results. It may take some time for one of your speeches to translate into business. But if you have given four speeches in the past year and they have not produced one "A-list" prospect, you may want to reconsider using speaking as a business development tactic.

When I asked one client to review the effectiveness of her marketing activities, she reported the following:

- She spoke at an American Bar Association mid-year meeting. The audience was comprise of about 100 lawyers in her specialty from around the country. It took 40 hours to research and prepare her speech, travel to the meeting, attend the meeting, and deliver the speech. A year later, it had not produced any results whatsoever.

- She had lunch with an existing client. It took three hours to set up the lunch, have the meal, and send a thank-you e-mail. As a result of the lunch, she was hired on a new matter.

- She wrote a white paper on new developments in Sarbanes-Oxley compliance, and e-mailed copies to about 50 clients and prospects with a short, personalized note highlighting why the issue might be of relevance to their business. It took her about sixteen hours to research and write the article, then draft the e-mails. As a result, several prospective clients called her and she was able to set up three lunches with them.

continued

Let's look at her results:

- Her most efficient and effective activity was having lunch with a client. It didn't take much time, and she got a new matter from her efforts.

- Her white paper was moderately efficient and effective. Although she spent a significant amount of time preparing and sending it, doing so moved her closer to being hired by several possible clients.

- Giving the speech at the conference was neither efficient nor effective. It took a lot of time, and to date, she hasn't received any new work for her efforts.

The activities that had the highest payoff involved drawing on personal, established relationships. The further away from that she ventured, the less efficient and effective her marketing.

Don't make the mistake some lawyers make—confusing marketing activity with marketing effectiveness. Look for those specific activities that actually produce results with the smallest investment of time.

A client of mine was devoting a lot of time to marketing. In the past year, she had:

- Founded the local chapter of an international association of lawyers in her practice area

- Organized four networking events for local businesswomen and the women lawyers in her firm

- Given two CLE programs for her local bar association

She felt frustrated that she'd devoted so much time to those activities, yet they hadn't brought in new business. Given that she had

continued

had been practicing law for 20 years, she had lots of names in her Rolodex. A more productive use of her time would have been to mine those existing relationships. She would have been better off setting up one-on-one meetings with past clients, sending articles with a thoughtful handwritten note to past referral sources, or visiting the offices of current clients.

Equally important, don't make the mistake of concluding that, because a particular time-consuming activity—such as heading up a practice group—produced a single piece of business, it's a high-payoff activity. The question to ask is this: if that same amount of time were invested in another type of business development activity, could it have produced a bigger return?

A client who is a bankruptcy lawyer organized several women's networking events, visited numerous prospects in far-off cities, and set up various in-house seminars for clients. She discovered that, despite her substantial external marketing efforts, the vast majority of her business came from referrals through two of her colleagues who had offices down the hall from her! She was able to redirect her energies to cross-marketing initiatives and get more business with less effort.

Rainmaking Action Steps

▶ List all the marketing activities you were involved in during the past year.

continued

TAP INTO YOUR TALENTS

To produce the best marketing results in the shortest period of time, focus on your business development strengths. When you engage in activities that play to your natural talents—whether that's talking or volunteering—you're more likely to do them. And when you take action, you get results. When those actions are based on your strengths, your results multiply.

Extensive research performed by the Gallup Organization and described in *Now, Discover Your Strengths* by Marcus Buckingham and Donald O. Clifton (Free Press, 2001), demonstrates that high achievement stems from exercising your strengths rather than improving your weaknesses. The biggest payoff will come from marketing activities that draw on the things you do best.

The concept of focusing on strengths and managing around weaknesses is, unfortunately, contrary to the conventional thinking in many law firms. The prevailing philosophy is that every lawyer can learn to be at least competent in almost anything and the greatest opportunity for growth comes from improving areas of weakness. This translates, for example, into encouraging lawyers who hate to give speeches to do it until it becomes more comfortable, or sending lawyers who hate attending networking events to training courses on how to be a better networker.

But, in reality, striving to overcome your weaknesses is a tremendous waste of energy. Performing activities that do not make the most of your natural skills drains your energy and rarely produces positive results.

Networking works best for those who enjoy meeting new people. Speaking works best for those who are energized by an audience. Quick e-mails and lunches are ideal solutions for those who enjoy building one-on-one relationships. Writing is a smart option for those who enjoy researching and putting pen to paper. Inviting clients to sporting events works well for those who like athletics and are a little uncomfortable making small talk.

In my years of working with successful rainmakers, I have seen a wide variety of effective approaches to business development, including:

- E-mailing contacts during a train commute
- Developing a strong network through participation in a local bar association
- Visiting clients at their places of business
- Writing for industry publications
- Team marketing with others in their firms
- Entertaining clients at theater events
- Seeking business from college friends who have become successful professionals
- Speaking to other practice groups in their firms
- Getting press in industry publications

Choose approaches that draw on your strengths. Any other approach simply takes too much effort and time. As the fitness expert Covert Bailey said about which exercise is best, "The one you will do!" In the end, Shakespeare's advice "to thine own self be true" is as valuable for those who are embarking on business development forays as it was for those embarking on travel abroad.

> **Rainmaking Action Steps**
> ▸ Reflect on your marketing activities during the past year. Which ones drew on your strengths?
>
> ▸ What other strengths do you have that you could incorporate into your marketing?

ARTICULATE YOUR STRENGTHS

"Knowing thyself" is not a simple task, so articulating your strengths can be elusive. It is likely that you take for granted your strengths because they come to you so naturally, leading you to believe that anyone can do them. Yet nothing could be further from the truth. For something to be valuable, it doesn't have to be difficult.

To help you articulate your business development strengths, consider these questions:

What business development activities energize you? Taking clients to lunch? Taking prospects to basketball games? Pitching a proposal to a client as part of a team? Attending networking events? Speaking before an industry group? These are likely to be your natural strengths.

What business development activities do you find draining? Taking clients out to lunch? Taking prospects to basketball games? Pitching a client as part of a team? You get the idea. These are activities to avoid, since they probably aren't your strengths.

What business development activities have people told you you're good at? Writing articles that bring a smile to the reader's face? Organizing client seminars? Selecting the perfect gift as a thank-you for a referral?

Another way to articulate your strengths is to look at the aspects of your practice, experiences, talents, or achievements that you can leverage in your marketing. Possibilities include:

Your clients. Do you have an impressive client list that includes many of the leading companies in the industry? Have you represented companies in a wide variety of industries?

Your client relationships. Do you have strong personal relationships with your clients? Are they loyal to you, always turning to you when they have a new matter? Are they great referral sources?

Your peer relationships. Are you highly regarded in the legal community? Are you well-respected by the other lawyers in your firm? Are you a team player who can recruit others to participate in your business-building activities?

Your practice area. Have you spent years developing expertise in a special niche, such as asset securitization or eminent domain law? Is your practice area hot right now?

Industry expertise. Have you developed expertise in a specific industry, such as telecommunications, because you've focused your practice on a narrow segment of the market? Can you draw on your background prior to becoming a lawyer, such as having been a reporter or a nurse? Is your past legal experience a plus, such as having been an Assistant U.S. Attorney?

Your reputation. Are you considered the go-to person for certain types of matters? Have you been ranked by Chambers or are you a member of the American College of Trial Lawyers? Have you held leadership positions in important bar committees? Have you been recognized for your contribution to important civic projects?

Reputation of your firm. Is your firm widely regarded as the go-to firm for specific issues, such as nuclear regulatory work or Supreme Court litigation?

Your visibility. Are you active in bar or community activities? Do people know you because of the leadership positions you have held? Do you have visibility in your niche, such as in the academic medical community?

Your network. Is your contact management system filled with the names of people who would quickly return your phone calls? Do you know lots of people at your biggest client? Have you religiously kept in touch with clients and former clients? Did you grow up in the community in which you are practicing? Are you active in your college or law school alumni activities? Do you have excellent relations with local judges?

Your marketing skills. Are you naturally strategic in the way you approach marketing? Have you organized your contacts into a system that allows you to identify individuals based on their specific interests? Are you disciplined in your approach to marketing? Are you persistent?

Your marketing support. Does your firm have an excellent marketing department that can support you in your efforts? Is your assistant a whiz at helping you follow up? Do you have an associate who's interested in learning marketing from you and is willing to support you in your efforts?

Your personal attributes. Are you naturally curious about other people? Do you have a strong client service mentality? Are you outgoing and great at making conversation, or are you quiet and a good listener? Do you have lots of interests besides practicing law? What others strengths do you have that you can leverage to make you more effective in business development?

Playing to your strengths can make business development more comfortable, more effective, more efficient, and even fun.

Rainmaking Action Steps

▶ Answer these questions:

   ▶ What business development activities energize you?

   ▶ Which business development activities do you find draining?

▶ List those aspects of your practice that you can use to bring in new business.

▶ Ask others what they see as your business development strengths. A coach can be very useful in helping you identify your strengths.

LEVERAGE YOUR STRENGTHS IN YOUR MARKETING EFFORTS

After determining your strengths, draw on them to make your marketing more effective and efficient. For example, let's say that one of your strengths is developing strong personal relationships with your clients. You can translate this talent into increased business in the following ways:

- Get together with existing and past clients on a regular basis.

- Focus your marketing on existing clients.

- Ask your clients for referrals to others who might benefit from your services (see Chapter 5 for the specifics on how to do this).

- Request that your clients meet with a colleague whose practice would represent an expansion of your firm's representation, but do so only after you're clear that the client needs the proposed services.

- End each telephone call with a short, personal conversation—asking about a new puppy or a daughter's progress in completing her college applications.

If one of your strengths is being a terrific public speaker, here are some ways to put that to work for you:

- Offer to speak at another practice group's brown-bag lunch to facilitate their cross-selling of your practice.

- Propose an in-house seminar on recent developments to your largest client.

- Make a presentation at the next industry conference and invite the trade press involved in that industry to cover your speech.

- Volunteer to speak at your firm's retreat to increase your visibility among your colleagues.

- Create a CD or MP3 of one of your recent speeches, and send it to your clients and prospects.

If you have an amazing network, you might:

- Introduce members of your network to each other at a lunch, cocktail party, or any social or professional gathering. They would probably enjoy and profit from these meetings, and if new relationships blossom, it will reflect well on you.

- Regularly keep in touch with members of your network through phone calls, e-mails, and networking events.

- Ask members of your network to introduce you to people they know whom you've targeted as potential clients.

- Solicit marketing advice from people in your network. Doing so could make them more invested in your success.

Rainmaking Action Steps

▶ Create a list of five ways to translate your personal strengths into specific marketing activities.

▶ Take a hard look at your marketing to-do list. Which activities draw on your strengths? Which ones don't? Cross off those that do not make the most of your strengths.

NURTURE YOUR EXISTING CLIENTS

Most lawyers get the vast majority of their new business from existing and past clients. These clients can be a source of new business by sending new matters and by making referrals.

Successful rainmakers know this. They recognize that existing clients are the most important people in their marketing mix, and they treat their current and former clients like the crown jewels of their practices.

Less successful rainmakers focus the lion's share of their marketing efforts on cultivating relationships with people with whom they have no prior business history. They ask these "strangers" to lunch. They invite them to their firm seminars. They call and send e-mails. Meanwhile, their most valuable assets, their existing clients, are being neglected.

> I was recently reminded of how easy it is to take your best clients for granted while working with a new client. We began our work together by looking at her list of clients, past and present. My client said, "We don't need to focus on this list; my clients are already a steady source of business. I know if they have a matter, they will send it to me."
>
> Nothing could be further from the truth.

Nurture your relationships with your clients, even when you are not doing work for them:

- Provide outstanding—not just good—service.
- Stay in touch on a regular basis—weekly, monthly, or quarterly.

- Ask for feedback on how you are doing, and act on the feedback you receive. One of the pet peeves of in-house counsel is that lawyers ask for feedback, but when they receive it, they do nothing with it. Don't make that mistake.

- Celebrate your client's successes. Send a gift recognizing a promotion. Host a bridal or baby shower.

- Take a client to a sporting or theater event just to say thanks for the business.

- Help make clients look good to their bosses or their in-house clients by crediting them with good ideas.

- Be responsive.

- Listen, really listen, to what they have to say. No multi-tasking while talking to a client.

- Provide advice off the meter.

- Learn about their business. Read their Web site. Ask about their company, products, and challenges.

- Keep them informed about the status of their matters.

- Support their favorite charities with your time or money.

- Help them—either on professional or personal issues.

- If you make a mistake, immediately acknowledge it and remedy it. Mistakes happen, but responding in a way above and beyond what is expected can build loyalty.

By making your clients the focus of your marketing efforts instead of devoting most of your time to strangers, you'll find marketing more rewarding. Your existing clients are your greatest assets. Treat them accordingly.

KNOW WHY YOU HAVEN'T BEEN HIRED (AND WHAT TO DO ABOUT IT)

Many lawyers engage in marketing activities that aren't a good match for the person to whom they're marketing because they haven't identified the obstacles to landing that specific client. Figuring out why you haven't been hired by a potential client can help you identify what your next marketing step should be. Start by asking this question: "Why haven't I been hired by this particular prospect?" The answer will vary by client, and depending on the response, different actions will be indicated.

Reasons for not getting hired include:

You don't know them. If you do not yet know who has a need for your services, do some research to identify precisely who your market is. Read trade journals. Attend industry meetings and targeted networking events, and ask questions. Do online research. Tap into your network to find out who might be a good prospect for you. Review your firm's client list for cross-selling possibilities.

They don't know you. You need to get on their radar screen. Perhaps you can ask a mutual friend to introduce you. You could moderate a panel and ask them to participate. You could get quoted in a publication they read. You could become active in an organization they belong to. You could give a speech at a venue they are likely to attend.

They don't know what you do. A lack of knowledge regarding the full spectrum of your services happens all too often. (If you doubt this, ask one of the lawyers in your firm what you do. You may be shocked to discover how little he or she knows.) It's time to educate these people. When they ask the inevitable question about what's new, reply with details highlighting a current project. Develop a good bragging speech, highlighting results you've achieved for your clients. Write an article on an area of expertise, and circulate it. Speak on an appropriate topic at a brown-bag lunch at your firm.

They don't like you enough. If you haven't yet built enough of a relationship for them to want to hire you, it's time to work on that. Make a point of asking a question about them at the beginning or end of each phone call, touching on both professional and personal topics. Add a few sentences to your e-mails that reflect your personality or interests. Invite them to lunch or to join you at a sporting event. Collaborate on a project together—whether it's for a bar committee or a local charity.

They don't trust you enough. Trust has to be earned, so ask to be referred by someone with whom the client has established a trusting relationship. Build your credibility by letting them know the types of matters you have handled in the past, the expertise you have acquired, and the successes you have achieved. Customize your bio so it focuses on how your accomplishments fit well with their needs. Invite them to a seminar where you're a presenter.

They don't know you want their business. Too often, busy lawyers share their "busy-ness" with their clients or prospects by telling them how overwhelmed they are. Potential clients interpret this as not wanting more business. There's a simple solution: stop talking about how busy you are and ask for business!

They don't have any business to give you. Lawyers often interpret not being hired by a prospect as rejection. More likely, it is because they don't have appropriate work to send your way right now. Stay on their radar screen. When they do have business, you'll likely be top of mind. Send staying-in-touch e-mails. Invite them to firm events. Call them periodically to check in. Send holiday cards. Go to networking events where they're likely to be. Send them articles of interest with a short note.

Once you figure out why you haven't been hired, you can focus on what you need to do to remove that obstacle.

Rainmaking Action Steps

▶ Determine why you haven't been hired by a client you'd like to land.

▶ Come up with a marketing strategy to overcome that problem.

CHAPTER THREE

Follow-Up

The biggest marketing mistake that lawyers make is failing to follow up. Too often, business development efforts are sporadic and inconsistent.

The main purpose of all your marketing activities—whether networking, meeting one-on-one, or speaking—is to identify people and issues appropriate for follow-up. When it comes to landing clients, follow-up is much more critical to your business development success than increasing your visibility or building your credibility.

> When I was a general counsel, I was puzzled by how little follow-up I saw. Typically, outside counsel, eager for my business, would invite me to lunch at a trendy restaurant, bring pricey marketing brochures, spend an hour extolling the virtues of their firm and their highly credentialed and experienced lawyers, ask for my business, and then disappear, never to be heard from again (or not for a year, at least).
>
> *continued*

> I now know what was going on. There was a lull in their client work or a sudden push for business development from within their firm, so they arranged to meet with me. The meeting went well, but I had no work to give them at the time. Then they got busy with client demands. When they resurfaced from their busy workload, they felt uncomfortable about contacting me again after so much time had passed. So they didn't. And the opportunity was lost.

BE CONSISTENT ABOUT STAYING IN TOUCH

Consider these factors to understand why consistent follow-up is so crucial:

- Clients can hire you only when they have a specific need for the type of services you provide. Unlike shoes or CDs, they hire lawyers only when they have an actual case or deal on their desk. So, before you can be hired, there must be a convergence of their having an appropriate matter and remembering you as someone who could help them with that matter.

- Research has shown that only three percent of all sales are made after the first contact. That means there's a 97 percent probability your first contact with a prospective client will not result in business.

- Research indicates that it takes an average of seven contacts before a sale is made. Eighty percent of all sales are made after the fifth contact. That means only 20 percent of all sales are made with fewer than five contacts.

- On average it takes seven to nine significant contacts to land a client.

Without consistent follow-up, the time you invest in business development is simply not likely to pay off. You need to stay in touch with prospective clients regularly. It's critical to remain on their radar screen so when the need for your type of services arises, your name immediately comes to mind.

Consistent follow-up is the key to effective marketing. If you aren't willing to invest the time, don't even bother with initial forays. Don't let great business development opportunities slip through the cracks because of failure to follow up.

Rainmaking Action Step
- ▶ Follow up today on the last marketing activity in which you engaged.

CREATE A GRAB BAG OF WAYS TO MAINTAIN CONTACT

If your follow-up is to be consistent, you need to identify a variety of ways in which you can execute it. Here are several ideas:

Send thank-you notes. Send an e-mail after you've met with a prospective client or talked at length on the phone, just to say thanks for the time spent with you.

Send articles. Choose something that you or others have written on personal or professional topics of mutual interest. Send a note with the article. Ask your librarian or an associate to keep an eye out for relevant articles.

Set up a meal. Arrange to have breakfast, lunch, coffee, dinner, or a drink together.

Send your firm's newsletter. Be sure to include a personal note highlighting an article of particular interest to your prospect.

Visit their offices. In my experience, this is a very effective way to get more business.

Call on the phone. Share ideas about professional or personal matters.

Forward links of interest. Send links to online articles or videos on topics of interest.

Offer to introduce them to others. Think about people they might be interested in knowing. It could be another client with whom they share common issues or concerns; it might be somebody they'd consider hiring as a professional organizer.

Invite them to events. These can be sports or cultural events. You're limited only by your interests and what you think might appeal to them.

Offer resources. Refer them to Web sites or blogs on topics of interest to them. Alert them to events, books, or podcasts they might find useful.

Ask for their advice. People love to give advice. If you're writing an article or giving a speech, ask, "Does this address the issues you're concerned about? Is it clear?" Inquire if they think attending a certain event is likely to be valuable to you. Ask for feedback on your marketing materials.

Ask what happened with your advice. Ask them how things turned out with the advice you gave them.

Send holiday cards. Mailing cards in December is an obvious choice, but think of other events to celebrate, too.

> **Rainmaker Action Step**
> ▶ Develop your own grab bag of ways you will follow up, and implement them.

CHAPTER FOUR

Build Strong Relationships

Relationships are at the core of successful business development. In all the talk about RFPs and articles and resumé building, this principle often gets lost.

Strong personal relationships create strong professional relationships. That's good news for women trying to build their books of business. Relationship building is a strength for most women—something they can leverage in their business development efforts.

Consider the following e-mail exchange between a male outside counsel and a male in-house counsel:

Male outside counsel: Good to see you at the bar dinner. If you ever need help with litigation, don't hesitate to ask.

Male in-house counsel response: It was good to catch up with you, too. I definitely know where to find you.

Can you imagine two women lawyers having that bare-bones exchange? Their exchange would sound more like this:

Female outside counsel: Jane, it was great to see you last night at the bar dinner. I really enjoyed the opportunity to catch up personally and professionally. I can't believe your daughter is in high school already. Trust me, the rocky road of adolescence will be over soon! Let's stay in touch.

Female in-house counsel: Mary, I really enjoyed the chance to catch up with you, too. Good to hear that your practice is going so well. I will definitely keep you in mind if we are in need of litigation help. Thanks for listening to me vent on teenage girls. I needed your optimistic perspective. Hope to see you again soon.

I received this e-mail from a client after her recent visit to a client:

"The trip last week went very well. While out of town to take a deposition, I stopped by to say hello to an existing client. Yesterday, the client called to let me know she had recommended me to her general counsel to take over a litigation matter for the company. I'm seeing how personal relationships are so important!"

LEARN ABOUT YOUR CLIENT'S BUSINESS

Surveys consistently indicate that clients want their outside counsel to learn more about their businesses. Here are several ways to do so:

- Read the trade and professional journals that serve their industry—anything from *Ad Age* to *The Painting and Coating Journal.*

- Join and participate in the trade associations to which they belong.

- Make it a practice to regularly review your clients' and prospects' Web sites.

- Ask your clients to add you to the distribution list for their companies' publicly available newsletters.

- Purchase and use your clients' or prospects' products (easier to do if your client manufactures razor blades than periscopes).

- Get regular online updates—such as Google® alerts—to learn about key personnel changes, product launches, and other news items.

- Interview professionals—consultants, accountants, and bankers—who serve the same clients to find out about their knowledge and experiences with those clients. Their perspective may give you a more complete picture of the companies with which you work—or want to work.

- Monitor case filings and government actions against your clients and prospects.

- Gather information directly. Ask your clients and prospects about the biggest challenges facing their businesses today. Talk about the current trends in their industries. Inquire where they expect their companies to be five years from now.

- Invite your clients to present a "reverse" seminar so they can describe their business to a group of your firm's lawyers who represent them.

Rainmaking Action Step

▶ Do at least one thing this week to learn more about your top three clients' businesses.

ASK QUESTIONS

The best marketing is client-focused—looking at the world through the eyes of the client or prospective client. To understand their world, you have to learn about them. The best way to do that is to ask questions—both about business life and life outside the office.

Asking questions can be a big challenge for many lawyers. As advisors and advocates, lawyers are used to being the person with the answers, not the person with the questions. Most lawyers are natural talkers—and for those who aren't, this may actually be a business development strength.

But by asking good questions and really listening to the answers, it's easy to learn a lot about your clients and prospective clients, build strong relationships, and figure out how you can help them.

Relationship building is about focusing on the client, not on yourself. Asking questions is a far more likely way to forge a relationship than talking. Make a point to ask appropriate questions, learn about others, and let them know you are interested in them.

Rainmaking Action Steps

▶ The next time you are heading off to meet with a client or prospective client, write at the top of your notepad: "Listen instead of talk."

▶ Consider questions you want to ask the next time you meet with a client or prospective client. Questions that begin with "Tell me about," "Describe," or "Why" are always good places to start.

FIND ALTERNATIVES TO GOLF-COURSE CONNECTIONS

Traditionally, a round of golf or an evening at a sporting event provides a vehicle for building business relationships. There's a lot to be said for these events as business development activities. You get to spend a lot of time together. You have a common experience to enjoy. You get to play together.

But many women lawyers don't enjoy playing golf or attending sporting events. Fortunately, other activities offer the same business-generating benefits:

Form a networking group. Your clients, prospects, and referral sources all have a need to build relationships with others who have similar interests. For example, let's assume you are a real estate lawyer. Commercial real estate brokers, lenders, and insurance brokers might profit from belonging to a group you formed to discuss commercial development issues in your area. You could make the group unique by offering something that existing trade associations don't address, such as an all-women's group or a group centered on a specific geographic area. The focus doesn't even have to be on business. For example, professional women who want to participate in a book club can fit the bill. You can get together for lunch or dinner on a regular basis. And it wouldn't hurt if you were the only lawyer in the group.

Organize an event—a dinner, cooking class, or walking tour. If starting an ongoing group seems too ambitious or too formal, bring together some of your clients and prospects for a one-time event—even better if your "matchmaking" results in business for your clients. Make sure you continue to follow up after the event.

Be a resource. Clients or prospects have all sorts of problems they need to solve. Some are business related, such as finding information for a presentation to senior management or finding a mid-level associate to hire for the company's in-house international practice. Others are personal, like finding a math tutor for their junior high schooler or a personal trainer for them. Helping them solve any kind of problem provides an important building block for developing a strong professional relationship.

Get personal. The strongest business relationships have both a professional and a personal component. To nurture them, recognize personal milestones—promotions, elections to leadership positions in trade or professional associations, legal victories—with a handwritten note. Better yet, send a carefully thought-out gift. The more individualized, the better. You could give an audiobook to someone who has a long commute, a book on disciplining toddlers to a beleaguered parent, or a new CD to a music lover who likes that particular artist. Your gift should reflect a sincere interest in them as people, not merely as clients.

Provide a clipping service. Ask your librarian to keep an eye out for articles about your clients and their companies. Send them a copy of an article they've written or in which they were quoted. Include a personal note congratulating them on their good press. Mail a copy of one of their company's ads, pointing out why you think it's so good. Doing these little things tells your clients you care about them *and* their businesses.

Enlist their help. People like to feel needed. Invite them to participate on a CLE panel you're organizing. Request feedback on the draft of an article you're writing. Ask for ideas about growing your business. By enlisting their help, you encourage people to invest in their relationship with you.

Coordinate plans. Take advantage of connecting with key clients and prospects at events you attend. For example, if you and a client or prospect serve on a board together or are planning to attend the same CLE program, use the opportunity to have lunch before or a drink afterwards. Even if the person declines your invitation, it reminds them that you're interested in building the relationship.

Do some personal PR. Self-promotion need not be uncomfortable. Send your clients and prospects copies of an article you wrote or in which you were quoted. Include a note pointing out the relevance of the article to their companies. Send brochures announcing an event at which you're speaking, and include a personal invitation to attend. They may not come, but doing this establishes you in their minds as an expert on the topic. Following your presentation, send your handouts to clients who weren't able to make it.

Volunteer together. Strategically select volunteer activities—those that will put you in contact with clients, prospects, and referral sources. Offer to serve on a committee for an organization to which your clients or prospects belong. It's even better if the committee can showcase the skills for which you'd like to be known. For example, if you're a tax lawyer, volunteer for the charitable giving committee. If you're an employment lawyer, help mediate a conflict between the board and the staff. You could also invite clients or referral sources to volunteer with you for an organization or cause of mutual interest—the local soccer league board, the legal aid society, or a Habitat for Humanity project.

Keep in touch. Out of sight is out of mind. To overcome that, you can organize an annual lunch with friends from law school, fellow judicial clerks, or alumni from your old law firm. They may not be able to send you business right now, but who knows where they'll be five years from now. Make a list of 50 to 100 people with whom you want to stay in touch on a regular basis. It can include former clients, former colleagues, or good referral sources. Make a commitment to contact them on a quarterly basis. (This is your "B list," which is discussed in Chapter 1.) You don't need an excuse to stay in touch other than to check in and ask how someone is doing. You can call from your cell phone while you're stuck in traffic, send an e-mail from your Black-Berry when you're waiting at the airport, or send a newsy holiday card (all the better if it's your family card and not the firm card). You can share news of a mutual friend. You can invite a colleague to join you for lunch to celebrate an event such as a birthday you share or the opening day of baseball season.

Building personal relationships with clients, prospective clients, and referral sources need not be a daunting task. Find ways to nurture relationships that are appropriate and comfortable for you. And never let your lack of golfing skills get in the way of developing important, business-building relationships.

> **Rainmaking Action Step**
> ▶ Pick one of the activities listed above and put it into action this week.

DON'T BE AFRAID TO GET PERSONAL

Don't be wary about personalizing your relationships with clients and prospects. If you don't establish strong personal relationships with them, you're much less likely to succeed in getting and keeping their business.

When I was an in-house counsel, my favorite outside counsel were people with whom I'd developed personal rapport. We appreciated the personal dimensions of each other's lives—whether we talked about movie or book recommendations, vacation adventures, or the challenges of private school admissions.

Many people are passionate about their hobbies—from gardening to decorating, from cycling to running, from wine collecting to salsa dancing. These provide great opportunities for conversation and connections.

For many people, their kids—or nieces or grandchildren—are central to their lives. Making the subject of kids taboo eliminates one of the fertile grounds for making connections. This is not to say that people want to hear about every dance recital or football victory, but never view sharing information about your out-of-office life as an off-limits topic.

> The most memorable gift I ever received from a client was an expensive stuffed animal when my second son was born. I would never have made such an extravagant purchase. But fifteen years later, I still remember it and its giver clearly. This gift for my son struck a personal chord and acknowledged an important event in my life.

Rainmaking Action Steps

▶ Share an aspect of your personal life with a client or prospect this week. Evaluate how it was received.

▶ Follow up by asking about a subject that has previously been shared with you—his son's role in the junior high musical or her recent trip to Italy.

MAXIMIZE YOUR VISIBILITY

One of the greatest myths in law firm life is that the lawyers in your firm will be eager to cross-sell your services just because they're your colleagues. But the fact is, they don't. Whether it's because of inertia, lack of knowledge of your capabilities, lack of incentives, fear of competition, or concern that you might negatively affect the relationship they have with "their" client, your colleagues cross-sell you less often than you might like.

Before people will refer work to you, they need to be clear about what you do. While it may seem that the other lawyers in your firm should know this, in reality, they likely don't. Firms are big places. Most of your colleagues only really know what you do when they work with you on a matter. Most of them are so busy thinking about their own reputations that they don't spend much time thinking about yours.

> A client of mine received an e-mail from one of her partners in another office. He was looking for a referral to a lawyer who did a specific type of hospitality-related financing deal. When she replied that she'd been doing similar work for many years, he was surprised. He had no idea she did that type of work.

The solution to this problem? Embark on an internal PR campaign. Like any good PR campaign, start by following these steps:

Be clear about your objectives. Know why you want increased visibility. To be included in the next marketing pitch? To have matters referred to you?

Be clear about what you want to be known for. Do you want to be seen as the go-to person for a certain type of transaction? That you have extensive experience in a specific industry? That you are great at finding creative solutions for difficult regulatory problems? Develop a clear message highlighting the reputation you want to have with your colleagues.

Focus on a specific audience. Who will you target with your message? The partners in your practice group? Those in the Corporate Group?

Once you've answered these questions, summarize your internal PR strategy into one sentence. For example: *I want to educate my colleagues in the IP group about my recent success in negotiating a complicated lease for a biotech company so they will refer their technology clients with real estate needs to me.*

The challenge, of course, is to raise your profile without, as one of my clients put it, "feeling sleazy." Consider using the following approaches:

Identify a few people you want to target and cultivate relationships with them. You might invite them to lunch or connect with them in the halls. Begin by asking questions about them, their practice, and their targets. That should lead to them asking questions about you. Take the opportunity to share the type of matters you'd like to handle. Emphasize why you're a safe choice for a referral. Be specific—tell them about cases you've handled and the good results you've achieved.

Share what you've learned in a recent successful case with others in your firm who might be interested. Send out an e-mail alerting your colleagues to circumstances that may raise issues for their clients. Suggest how the risk can be managed. Tie your advice to your recent experience (read: success).

Offer to speak at other practice groups' meetings. Make sure your presentation focuses on issues that are useful to them—something they can pass along to their clients and look good. Give them a checklist they can easily forward to their clients.

Get the word out. If your firm has a structure for publicizing successes—through an in-house newsletter, your practice group, or the marketing department—take advantage of it to educate others about your victories.

Offer to present at all-firm or all-practice group events. Again, make sure your comments are relevant to the participants, and focus on something for which you want to be known.

Rainmaking Action Step

▶ Raise your profile in your firm by developing a PR campaign that informs your colleagues about what you do and how well you do it. Have a clear message and a targeted audience for that message.

CHAPTER FIVE

Ask for Business

Many people can help you generate business—clients, colleagues, classmates, consultants, opposing counsel, people in your network, and even friends. But to make the most of the opportunities that these relationships present, you must take the initiative and ask for business.

Asking for business is one of the most commonly mentioned business development challenges faced by lawyers, but it needn't be daunting or unsavory. The key to doing it successfully is to spend time discovering your clients' needs before attempting to convince them to hire you. Many lawyers assume they know what their clients' needs are, so they don't take the time to explore them thoroughly. But in reality, they may be off track.

A client of mine assumed that, because it was widely reported in the press that her client was on a buying spree for California real estate, they were in need of California real estate counsel. So she pitched her firm's real estate services. However, the company already had what they considered to be excellent counsel, and they weren't interested in considering her. By asking the client about his needs instead of assuming them, she would have saved everyone valuable time.

Had the lawyer touting her firm's real estate services done her homework, she might have discovered that her client had other problems with which her firm might help. In this case, one of the properties the client purchased had significant environmental contamination, and they needed advice about their insurance options. If she had taken the time to discover this need, she could have told her prospect about her firm's specialized insurance coverage practice, and she might have received that business.

UNCOVER YOUR CLIENT'S NEEDS

Suppose you would like to represent a particular company. You meet the assistant general counsel of that company at an industry function, and he agrees to have lunch with you. Now what?

Here's what not to do: Don't go in selling. Don't bring the firm's brochure. Don't take one of your partners who might be able to sell him something else. It's too early to do any of that.

Your task is to ask lots of questions so you can find out what his needs are. Asking questions and listening closely to the answers before attempting to sell has several advantages:

- You save yourself the embarrassment and inefficiency of selling something the prospect isn't buying.

- You could discover a great opportunity.
- You demonstrate your sincere interest in the client.

How do you go about discovering a client's needs? It depends on which of these two circumstances you are in:

Scenario 1: You're meeting with a prospective client. You don't know what his needs are or if you could be of service. (This might occur with someone you met at a networking event, who has agreed to sit down with you.) Your questions should be broad enough to gather the big picture of his industry, organization, and possible legal needs. You might use the following openers to find out about his potential needs and the opportunities for you:

- Tell me about your company, its products, customers, competition, and growth opportunities.
- How's business?
- Tell me about your background.
- What attracted you to join the company?
- What is the most difficult thing about your job?
- What are your biggest challenges?
- If you could get one thing off your desk, what would it be?
- What are your company's legal hot spots?
- Tell me about your legal department.
- Describe your in-house legal team.
- How do you split your in-house/outside counsel responsibilities?
- How do you decide which outside counsel to use?

- What is the most important thing to you when you hire outside counsel?
- What is your biggest frustration in dealing with outside counsel?
- What firms do you currently use and for what?
- How satisfied are you with your current representation?
- What do you know about our firm?
- Do you think there is an opportunity for us to work together?

Scenario 2: The prospective client has contacted you to discuss a specific legal need, such as proposed litigation, an acquisition, or a compliance audit. In this case, your questions will be considerably more focused. Before attempting to convince her to hire you, make sure you understand her situation fully by asking questions such as:

- What prompted your call?
- How did you come to call us?
- Tell me about your current situation.
- What is your most immediate need?
- What have you done so far?
- What impact will it have on your company if this problem is not resolved or this deal doesn't happen?
- What would you like to see happen?
- What criteria are important to you in making a decision about hiring outside counsel?
- Who else is involved in the decision-making process?
- When do you expect to make a decision?

In either scenario, you'll want to have a thorough understanding of how the client perceives his or her situation before you make your sales pitch. Once you're confident that you have a clear understanding of the situation, you'll be able to formulate a more convincing presentation of your abilities and the value you could add.

> **Rainmaking Action Steps**
> ▶ Before the next meeting where you plan to ask for business, prepare a list of questions to make sure you understand what the client is interested in buying.
>
> ▶ Get the answers to these questions before asking for business.

ALWAYS AGREE ON THE NEXT STEP

You thoroughly comprehend the client's needs and have made a compelling presentation about your ability to meet those needs. Now what?

Before leaving the meeting, agree on the next step. This should be an agreement to take a specific action within a specific time frame. Many lawyers get tripped up during this stage because of the following pitfalls:

There is no agreed-upon next step. They leave the meeting with no plan for future action. Who will contact whom? When?

The next step is not specific enough. The client says something like, "I'll take a look at your materials and get back to you." Or, "Let me discuss it with our general counsel." But there is no specific time frame for what will happen when.

The ball is left in the prospect's court. As in the example above, the next step is entirely up to the prospect. It will happen, if at all, when he decides to do something. The lawyer asking for business has lost control of the process.

You can avoid these pitfalls by ending the meeting with questions such as:

- Where should we go from here?

- How would you like to proceed?

- It would be great to work with you. How can we make that happen?

- I think I have a pretty good idea of your situation, and I'm sure we can help you achieve your goals. What's our next step?

- Is this something you would like to move forward with?

- Here's what I recommend. How does that sound?

- What additional information do you need to make a decision?

- Would you be interested in receiving a proposal?

- Would you like to see a proposed budget?

- Do I need to meet with anyone else? How should I go about setting up that meeting?

- Would you like to meet with my partner? When would be a good time?

- I can see you don't have a need right now. Would it be ok to contact you again in six months?

- I have a recent brief/article/checklist relating to the topic we discussed. Would you like me to send it to you?

Make sure you remain in control of the next step. Ask the prospect if it would be OK for you to follow up if you haven't heard from him within a specific time frame. And, as with all aspects of business development, follow-up is key. If the prospect agreed to get back to you in two weeks and you haven't heard from him, call him. If you agreed that you would be back in touch in six months, do it.

Asking for business doesn't have to be intimidating. With a clear understanding of a prospect's needs, the "ask" can be the logical next step in the conversation.

> **Rainmaking Action Steps**
> ▶ Never leave a marketing meeting without a clear next step that is within your control.
>
> ▶ Always follow up on the agreed-upon next step.

ASK FRIENDS FOR BUSINESS

One of my clients once observed that the last person a woman will ask for business is her best friend. But friends can be an important source of business. It's a shame to write them off just because of your personal relationship.

My clients often say things like, "My best friend from college just went in-house at a financial services firm. I'm reluctant to ask for business because she'll think I'm taking advantage of our friendship." Or, "A good friend is a senior executive at a major franchisor. I'd like to get an introduction to the legal department there, but I just don't feel comfortable asking for that favor."

Reluctance to ask a friend for business boils down to a concern that by mixing business with friendship, it will spoil the friendship. The remedy for this dilemma is found half in mindset and half in tactics.

Consider the following:

Your friend is faced with a serious problem. Nobody hires a lawyer just for fun. If her company is embroiled in a situation that requires legal assistance, who better to come to her aid than you? After all, you have a vested interest in her success and welfare.

Your friend is used to being asked for business. If she's in a position to hire legal counsel, she's a savvy businessperson—someone who knows that others need to market their services (she might even ask for business more than you do). She won't be offended by your approach. In fact, she may wonder why you waited this long to talk about it.

You're a competent lawyer. What's the likelihood that something will go so wrong that it destroys the friendship? Have you considered that working together might even deepen your friendship? Your friend gets to see another dimension of you in an area where you shine. Besides, working with friends can be fun.

You shouldn't take it personally. If your friend doesn't hire you, it's probably because she doesn't have a need for your services right now or is not in a position to hire you. It doesn't mean that she won't hire you in the future or that she doesn't respect you as a professional.

Once you have the right mindset, you're ready to ask her for business. Here's a way you might accomplish that:

"Elizabeth, I would like to talk about the possibility of our doing business together, but I don't want to impinge on our friendship. Could I come to your office on Tuesday and discuss your legal needs? I'd like to see if there's an area where my firm or I might be able to help your company."

This approach has three advantages:

- It clearly acknowledges that you value the friendship.

- It lets your friend know you recognize the boundaries between friendship and business, and makes it clear that you do not intend to convert your time together into an endless barrage of sales pitches.

- It puts you on a businessperson-to-businessperson footing when discussing business.

Have you overlooked any friends as potential prospects for your services? If so, it's time to get over your reluctance to ask for their business. With the right mindset and approach, doing business with friends can be fun and profitable.

Rainmaking Action Steps

▶ Showcase your "business self." Invite your friend to your office, to an event sponsored by your firm, or ask for business advice.

▶ Make a list of three friends—in-house lawyers or business executives—who could either send you business or introduce you to someone who might be able to send you business.

▶ Use the approach suggested to ask for business or for a referral.

REQUEST REFERRALS

Referrals are a great source of new business. In fact, other than getting more work from existing clients, they are the most efficient and effective way to get new business.

Referrals are so effective because they make it easier to build the trust that is so critical in selling legal services. The referral source trusts you, the prospective client trusts the referral, and *voila!*—that trust is transferred to you.

Yet most lawyers don't actively seek the referrals that would make the sales process go much more smoothly. Referrals are a vast, untapped marketing gold mine for most lawyers.

Most lawyers assume that if a satisfied client or good friend hears of someone who might need their services, the client or friend will mention them. This happens less often than you would like. After all, most people are so busy thinking of their own careers that they have little time to think about yours.

Even for those lawyers who do ask for referrals, the typical (and largely ineffective) request goes something like this: "If you hear of anyone who needs my services, I hope you'll keep me in mind."

There are at least two problems with this phrasing:

- The person being asked is probably a busy professional with a lot on his plate. Keeping someone in mind for a referral is not a very high priority for him.

- The person being asked probably doesn't have a clear idea of what a good referral for you would look like, even if she were inclined to help.

Instead of using a vague request, try asking for exactly what type of referral you'd like. Create as vivid a picture as possible of what that referral might look like.

An effective "ask" has the following elements:

A clear statement describing the type of clients you're seeking. It's important that your potential referral source know what kind of clients would be appropriate referrals for you. The more specific you can be, the better. Do you have the name of someone you'd like to meet? Can you describe the person's position, such as the CEO of a hospital or the general counsel of an advertising agency? Can you outline specific scenarios in which someone might need your services, such as someone who has recently constructed a building and is less than happy with the workmanship, or someone who is starting a new venture in the nanotechnology industry?

> My client, an ESOP lawyer, developed a clear picture of who would be a great referral for her: "My ideal client is a family-owned company transferring the business to the next generation, and looking for a way to pay the founder a fair price for his stock without having to sell the company to a third party." With this description, she didn't have to go into esoteric detail about ESOPs—a listener would know the type of referral that would make sense for her.

A clear statement of the help you'd like. Again, the clearer you are about what you want, the more likely it is that you'll get it. Do you want to be introduced to a specific person? Would you like the referral source to set up a lunch for the three of you? Do you want her to send an e-mail introducing you? Do you want her OK to use her name when calling? Do you want to know who else she knows who might need your services?

> One of the members of my Women Rainmakers Roundtable represents lawyers and law firms. Her specific and effective "ask" was to request that members of her Roundtable forward an invitation to a seminar sponsored by her firm to the managing partners at their law firms. Because it was so specific and easy to do, many people agreed to help.

My favorite way to construct your "ask" is to say something like, "If you were in my shoes and were interested in growing your practice (e.g., among real estate developers in Boston), how would you go about doing it?"

This "ask" is effective because it's easy for you to deliver and it's comfortable for the person being asked. If he is not interested in helping or can't help, he'll say so, change the subject, and move on. If he is interested in helping, not only will he give you great ideas, but he will often offer to assist by giving you specific names or making a call on your behalf.

Referrals can be the key for growing your practice, if only you *ask!*

Rainmaking Action Steps

▶ Ask someone for a referral this week.

▶ Describe the kind of person or business to whom you'd like to be referred.

▶ Be clear about what you're asking the possible referral source to do.

ASK TO BE CROSS-SOLD

You can't assume that the other lawyers in your firm will automatically cross-sell your services. Instead, you will need to take the initiative and ask to be cross-sold. To launch your campaign, follow these steps:

Identify no more than five colleagues who present good cross-selling opportunities for you. Evaluate them based on the focus of their practices, their client base, and, most important, their willingness to cross-sell. Realize that some people are eager to do so, while others simply aren't. Life is too short to try to convert them.

Develop a relationship with each of the people you've identified. Get to know each individual on a personal level—through conversations in the hall, having lunch, or working together on a client matter.

Educate them about what you do. As surprising as it may seem, most people, even the lawyers in your firm, don't know what you really do. They may have a general idea—you are an antitrust lawyer—but they may not understand that you specialize in Hart-Scott-Rodino filings. So your task is to educate them about the breadth and depth of your practice.

Inform them how well you do what you do. Not all the lawyers in your firm are equally talented, equally smart, equally client-oriented, and equally diligent. To convince your colleagues that they can entrust their clients to you, share your successes with them and let them know how delighted your clients are with the service you provide.

Make your expectations clear. Don't assume that your colleagues know to whom you want to be cross-sold and for what services. Explain your game plan to them: "I think there is an opportunity for your client "X" to hire us to do "Y" type of work, which I do. Can we sit down and develop a plan for how we might go about doing that?"

Make it clear what's in it for them. Most people are motivated by self-interest. To encourage your colleagues to act on your behalf, highlight the benefits to them. These will vary depending on the situation. Perhaps it will strengthen the client relationship. Maybe it will be viewed positively by the firm's leadership. Or you might agree to share the billing credit.

If you want to be cross-sold, approach your efforts to market to your colleagues with the same focus and seriousness as marketing to potential clients.

Rainmaking Action Steps

▶ Identify no more than five lawyers in your firm who are good candidates to cross-sell you based on their willingness to cross-sell, their practice, and their client list.

▶ Develop a specific game plan to get them to cross-sell you.

▶ Be up front about what your colleagues have to gain from cross-selling you. How do you propose that the credit be shared? How will you manage the matters so they won't worry that their client relationship will be compromised?

CHAPTER SIX

Make Time to Market Your Practice

When I ask women lawyers to name their biggest marketing challenge, the response I hear most often is "Finding time to do it."

The stark reality is that you'll never *find* time to market. You have only 24 hours in every day and seven days in every week. You're probably already overbooked and perhaps overwhelmed with all the commitments you have. So it's not really a question of *finding* time; it's about *making* time for business development by making it a priority.

As this chapter will demonstrate, making time for business development is as much about developing a marketing mindset as it is about time management. When you make time, your rainmaking activities move to the top of your to-do list, and you treat them with the same respect you treat client commitments. You recognize how critical it is to spend time on business development to help ensure your future success.

How much time you spend on this year's billings will determine your salary. How much time you spend on business development will determine your future. So invest in tomorrow by making time for business development today.

ADOPT A MARKETING MINDSET

Not all marketing activities must be time consuming. In fact, marketing opportunities abound in your daily e-mails, phone conversations with clients, and hallway chats with others in your firm. The trick is to develop a mindset that recognizes and capitalizes on these opportunities when they come your way. Look for ways to turn your daily interactions into marketing activities.

Take a look at how the lack of a marketing mindset can lead to missing significant marketing opportunities:

Several years ago, I spoke at a law firm's women's retreat. One objective of the retreat was for participants to get to know each other better to facilitate cross-selling. People flew in from all over the country for this three-day event. It was a huge time commitment for the attendees.

As part of the retreat program, the marketing department put together a directory that included each attendee's bio. Each woman was asked to fill out a questionnaire that included the following questions:

continued

> - What excites you about your practice?
>
> - What's the most interesting thing you've been working on?
>
> - What are your interests outside of the law?
>
> I'm guessing it would have taken about five minutes to complete the questionnaire—a tiny fraction of the time invested in attending the retreat. The responses could have provided a basis for starting conversations with the other attendees and facilitated cross-selling. Unfortunately, about two-thirds of the attendees failed to fill out the questionnaire. They missed a golden opportunity to have others get to know them better, begin to build relationships, and develop contacts for cross-selling.

Here are several ways to convert day-to-day tasks into marketing opportunities:

- At the end of every conversation you have with a client, work on building the relationship. Inquire about the person's business. Ask questions such as:
    - "What impact are the reports about recent SEC investigations having on your businesspeople?"
    - "How is that search for a new administrative assistant going?"

Or ask a personal question:

- "How was your vacation in Belize?"
- "How did your daughter's team do at the speech and debate tournament?"

You might also share a personal story about yourself, such as a book you've read recently or a play you've seen.

- When you meet at a client's office, use the opportunity to reconnect with people you know there. Take five minutes to walk around and say hello to colleagues with whom you've worked before.

- Before attending your next partners' meeting, think about which individual you'd like to have cross-sell your services. Make a point of sitting next to that person at lunch so you can get to know each other better.

- At the end of a transaction, focus on the question "Was there anything I learned in this matter that might be of interest to other clients?" If so—and if it's not confidential—send out a quick e-mail sharing your insights with other clients.

- When a matter ends, call your client to tell them how much you enjoyed working with them.

- Each day, while reading the newspaper or an online news service, look for an article that's appropriate to send to a client or prospect. Send it or forward it with a brief note highlighting why you think it might be of interest to them.

- When you travel for business, determine those clients or referral sources with whom you can meet while you're there. Schedule lunch or a late-afternoon drink. Even if you don't manage to get together, at least you made contact with the person.

- When you attend a conference or continuing legal education program, don't spend the breaks checking your BlackBerry or calling your office. Instead, use the opportunity to meet new people. It's easy to connect with others in this environment because you're all there for the same reason and most people don't know the other attendees. If you're looking for a conversation starter, referring to the previous presentation is a natural.

- Build relationships with co-counsel and opposing counsel. For example, use the breaks during depositions to develop relationships with attorneys in different states who might become referral sources. Conduct yourself as someone whom those attorneys would want to hire if the opportunity presented itself.

- Showcase yourself in the best possible light when given the opportunity. Be thoughtful about how you fill out biographical questionnaires, emphasizing what you want people to know about you.

- Develop a good answer to "What's new?" and make sure it highlights you and your practice. (See Chapter 7 for details on how to do this.)

- Schedule client meetings at a time when it would be natural to have lunch or a glass of wine afterwards. Taking time off the clock to get to know clients or prospects is one of the key contributors to strong relationships.

Even the time-starved can dramatically increase their marketing effectiveness by adopting a marketing mindset in their daily activities.

Rainmaking Action Step
▶ Sharpen your marketing mindset and look for five marketing opportunities, no matter how small, in your everyday encounters this week.

DEVELOP GOOD HABITS

It's difficult to market on a consistent basis unless you have a system in place for when you will market. The goal is to develop marketing habits that are so natural and automatic that you don't even have to think about them.

It's a lot like exercising. My experience is that those who are successful at exercising set aside a regular and specific time and place to do it. Some exercise in the morning. Others go to the gym in the evening after work three times a week. Some play tennis on Tuesday nights. Few successful exercisers decide on an ad hoc basis each morning whether or not they'll exercise that day.

The same applies to marketing. To do it consistently, you need to develop a habit or system. Such systems can vary as much as the individuals devising them, but they are systems nonetheless. Setting up a workable marketing schedule will serve you and your marketing goals well.

Consider these habits:

- Some lawyers spend the first 15 minutes of each day on rainmaking activities. They come into the office, get their coffee, and set to work on marketing tasks. That's enough time to pick up the phone and arrange a lunch, send someone an e-mail about a recent development, ask a librarian to look for articles about a new prospect, or think about whom to call during the next month. They devote a quarter of an hour, day in and day out. This consistency produces results.

- One of my clients visits a different client each month. She uses the plane trip home to plan how she'll follow up during the rest of the year with the client she just visited.

- One of my clients belongs to several networking groups and attends their monthly meetings religiously. Because it's on her calendar, she goes. Then she commits to following up with at least one person she meets at each meeting.

- Another of my clients checks in with her major clients every Friday. She asks, "How're you doing? Anything we can help you with? Are we getting you what you need?" Then she follows up with them on personal matters, as well. This routine has become so systematized that if she fails to call on a Friday, her clients actually call her to check in.

- Another client buys season tickets to the theater and commits to taking a client to each show. (She's made a pact with herself not to give the tickets to her assistant or to the associate down the hall.) A similar strategy could work with sports or lecture tickets. Just make sure to extend your invitation well in advance. If you call at the last minute, your client might think you're simply trying not to waste a ticket.

- Another client habitually goes to lunch every Wednesday with a client or prospect who is a target in her business plan.

- One client devotes four hours on the third Wednesday of the month entirely to business development. She blocks it off on her schedule as though she is out of town.

- Another client makes five staying-in-touch phone calls a week. She doesn't go home at the end of the week until those calls have been made. (If you'd never get around to calling five people, make your goal less ambitious—call three people or even one. Do the math—if you call one person a week, you've made fifty contacts in a year, which is definitely better than none.)

As you set up your system, be sure to account for the inevitability that you'll experience times when you are too busy to market. Still, figure out at least one small commitment you can make to business development (for example, sending out one staying-in-touch e-mail each day), even when you're swamped. Treat these commitments to connect as seriously as you would a promise you've made to a client.

Rainmaking Action Steps

▶ Cultivate a specific marketing habit. Try it for a month, and then assess how it's working. If your first idea doesn't work, try another one until you come up with a system that works for you.

▶ Keep your marketing habits simple. Aim for three things that you do consistently—for example, spending 15 minutes on marketing three times a week, visiting people when you're out of town, and hosting a weekly marketing lunch.

▶ Schedule your marketing habit on your calendar until it becomes automatic. Hold it inviolate.

INVEST YOUR TIME IN THE RIGHT PLACES

How much time do you realistically have to devote to business development? Being honest about the time you have to commit is key to making sure you invest it in the right places.

Figure out how many hours you can truly devote to marketing by answering these questions:

- How much time did you spend on business development in the last year?

- Have circumstances changed so you're likely to have either more or less time to spend on marketing in the year ahead?

- What activity on your current agenda can you eliminate to make additional time for business development? Perhaps you can resign from some administrative activities that are not helping you build your book of business, such as the Summer Associate Committee, the Associate Evaluation Committee, or the Hiring Committee. (See the end of this chapter for ideas on how to say "no.") Maybe you can delegate some legal, administrative, or business development tasks that are currently taking up your time.

Once you have determined how many hours you can realistically spend on business development, it becomes a filter through which you can measure whether any given activity is a good use of your limited marketing time.

Say you have decided to commit 100 hours a year to business development. You get a call inviting you to speak at a PLI conference in a distant city. Giving a speech typically takes about 40 hours, when you factor in the time to research the topic, write the speech, prepare the PowerPoint and handouts, travel to and from the event, give the speech, attend the conference, and follow up. Ask yourself if that 40 hours is a good investment of time when you have only 100 hours total for business development. Is it worth 40 percent of your available marketing time?

To help you determine the answer, ask these questions:

- What results have you received from similar events in the past?

- How else could you spend that time? If a typical lunch with a client takes three hours, perhaps setting up a dozen lunches with existing clients and referral sources is a better use of your time than accepting this invitation to speak.

- Will this activity help you achieve the results you want in the most efficient and effective way possible?

> **Rainmaking Action Steps**
>
> ▶ Figure out how much time you realistically have to devote to your marketing efforts. Can you find more time by eliminating time-consuming, unproductive aspects of your practice, such as serving on committees?
>
> ▶ Every time you contemplate a business development activity that takes a significant amount of time—whether it is responding to an RFP, writing an article, or attending a conference—estimate how long it will take, what percentage of your available marketing time that represents, and whether it is a good investment of the time you have available.

BE CLEAR ON YOUR MOTIVATION

To make business development a priority worthy of your time, you must be clear on your motivation for being a successful rainmaker. Why do you care about bringing in business, anyway?

When I ask lawyers this question, they often give answers like:

- "I want to contribute to my firm."
- "There is a lot of pressure to bring in new work."
- "It's what partners should do."

Although those reasons may be laudable, they rarely motivate anyone to attend an after-hours dinner with clients instead of heading home to family or other activities. No wonder lawyers struggle to maintain momentum in their business development efforts.

To build your own marketing motivation, develop a compelling and personal reason for why *you* want to have your own book of business. Get crystal clear on what reaching your business development goals will do for you. Understand that being successful at business development means different things to different people. It's very personal.

Here are some of the reasons my clients have given for why they want to develop their own books of business:

- "It will increase my compensation. That additional money will fund something important to me, like taking my family on an African safari or making a significant contribution to my favorite charity."

- "I'll be rewarded with a place on one of the firm's important committees. Perhaps I'll be appointed to the Management Committee, where I can advocate for the changes I believe are critical to the firm's future."

- "I'll have more say about the clients and colleagues with whom I work and on what kinds of matters I work on. I won't have to deal with difficult people or spend time on matters I find boring."

- "I'll have a portable book of business. I'll have options in my career, and that's important to me."

- "I'll feel more secure. I'll sleep better at night knowing I won't have to worry about my fate in the next round of partner de-equitizations."

- "I'll have less billable-hour pressure. I can have a more flexible schedule that might allow me to coach my daughter's soccer team or participate in outside activities of importance to me."

Each of these reasons is specific and personal—that's why they're motivating. Once you've created your own compelling vision, you're likely to be much more enthusiastic about marketing.

Whenever you find yourself putting off those business-building activities, remind yourself about the impact that being a successful rainmaker could have on your life. That should inspire you to keep moving toward your goals.

Rainmaking Action Step

▶ Take a few minutes to envision why growing your book of business is important to you. Make it as personal and vivid as possible. Write down your motivations for being successful at business development, and put it in a place where it's visible to you every day.

CALCULATE THE VALUE OF A NEW CLIENT

If you can't find time for business development activities, maybe you aren't convinced about the value of a new client. Once you become clear about that, marketing activities might move to the top of your to-do list.

It may sound ludicrous to suggest that you don't know the value of a new client. But have you taken it from the abstract—*it's good to bring in business*—to the concrete, calculating the dollar value of a new client or matter?

Of course, the new client's value depends on the size of potential billings and the likelihood of repeat business. But regardless, the value of any new client is substantial.

So before you decide to have lunch at your desk instead of with a referral source, or skip going to a client's office when you're in another city so you can catch an earlier flight home, calculate the value of a new client or new matter by considering the following:

- If you were to get work from this client or referral source, how much revenue would it likely produce?

- Would having this client on your client roster enhance your reputation and credibility with others? Will a new matter for this client broaden or deepen your expertise or experience in a way that you can leverage in future marketing efforts?

- How likely is it that this new client will generate repeat business over the course of the relationship?

- If the new client does send repeat business, how much revenue might that produce?

- How does this additional origination credit translate into more compensation for you?

- What is the probability that this new client will refer you to others in their network who might do business with you?

You're probably thinking, "It's not that simple. Not every lunch results in new business." Agreed. But if the lunch is with a well-qualified prospect and not a "random act of lunch," there is some probability that it will do so. What if there's a ten percent probability that the meeting will produce new business? Even with that small probability, the value of the lunch can be substantial.

Let's assume the value of the new matter generated by the potential client is a modest $50,000. If there is a ten percent possibility that that lunch will land a new client, the value of the lunch is $5,000. And that doesn't take into account the value of the possible repeat business or referrals or the resumé enhancement that the business might provide.

When viewed in this way, how can you afford *not* to go to that lunch?

Rainmaking Action Step

▶ The next time you're tempted to pass on a well-targeted business development opportunity—whether it's writing a personal note on your holiday cards or going out to dinner with a client—calculate the probable long-term value of that relationship and decide if it's worth investing the time in marketing to that person.

JUST SAY "NO"

A great way to make time for business development is to say "no" to non-essential, non-strategic activities—those that consume time but don't help you build your practice. These activities typically fall into three main categories: administrative roles in your firm, non-targeted speaking and writing activities, and RFPs and client pitches that have not been properly vetted for the probability of success.

It's flattering to be asked to serve on your firm's committees or be a featured speaker at a conference, but first ask yourself these questions:

- How much time will the activity take?
- How satisfying will it be?
- Will it help you grow your book of business?
- Will it move you toward the practice you want to have?
- Who else could do it?
- Are you doing more than your fair share?

In most firms, rainmaking success is much more highly valued than administrative contributions. However, the time you have available to invest in business development comes from the same pot of non-billable hours as administrative responsibilities.

Women lawyers, in particular, seem to have a difficult time balancing the requests of others with the need to invest their limited non-billable time in the ways most likely to grow their practices. This push-pull is compounded by the unfortunate fact that the relatively small number of senior-level women in a firm are often asked to serve as "the representative woman" on various administrative committees. Yet learning to say "no" is necessary if you're committed to protecting your limited marketing time.

My client, a rising star in her law firm, was asked to serve on every conceivable committee because she had a reputation for being smart and getting things done. It's no exaggeration to say that she served on about a dozen committees within her firm.

She decided that if she were to reach her goal of having a significant book of business, she'd need to refocus her energies. She resigned from all her committee assignments and, within three years, was among the firm's top-billing lawyers.

Turning down offers to serve on prestigious and not-so-prestigious committees may not be simple. The person asking may be someone with whom you're trying to nurture a relationship. Perhaps you're concerned that you won't be viewed as a team player if you're not willing to serve in the offered role. Perhaps you think that the role will position you to better market your practice within and outside the firm.

But the truth is, I have never seen a lawyer whose book of business did not benefit more from investing time in business development than in committee work, no matter how high-powered the committee. The notion that enhanced stature in the firm will translate into new business is rarely true.

In her book *Civilized Assertiveness for Women: Communication with Backbone . . . Not Bite* (Albion Street Press, 2007), Judith Selee McClure, PhD, offers suggestions on how to say "no" in a way that preserves your relationships and positions you positively in the eyes of others. I've adapted her suggestions to help you say "no" to protect your valuable marketing time:

The "No, Because": "I'd like to help you on the Recruiting Committee, but I've spent a lot of time developing a focused marketing plan, and I promised myself that this year I would use my non-billable time to execute it." Saying "no" for this reason may actually elicit respect rather than disapproval.

> One of my clients recently used the "no, because" with the Managing Partner of her firm when he invited her to join a highly visible administrative committee. His response? "I agree. Doing business development is a much better use of your time than serving on that committee."

The "Partial No": "I can't chair the Summer Associates Committee, but I'd be glad to have lunch with the summer associates three times during the summer." Or, "I can't help you draft that RFP, but I'd be glad to review and comment on your draft."

The "Not Now No": "No, I can't give that speech to the local bar association this year, but please keep me in mind for next year when my schedule may have eased up a bit."

The "Alternative No": "No, I don't have time to write the practice group description, but I think that would be an excellent project for one of our senior associates who has shown an interest in getting more involved in business development. I think this would be a great chance for her to get her feet wet."

The "Just Plain No": "I'm flattered that you considered me for the position as head of the Associate Evaluation Committee. At the moment, I just don't have time to do it justice."

If you want to have time for business development, you have to learn to say "no." Refer to these options as a way to protect your valuable marketing time. You'll be perceived as someone who has a clear sense of priorities and is committed to growing her practice. Prepare to be amazed at the results you can achieve when you make time for business development by eliminating non-strategic activities.

> **Rainmaking Action Steps**
> ▶ Practice saying "no" to the next request you get to be involved with a non-strategic activity. Explain that you're investing your non-billable time in business development efforts this year. Saying "no" gets easier with practice.
>
> *continued*

- ▶ If you are afraid to say "no" to a request, seriously consider what is the worst thing that will happen if you do. Frequently, you'll realize your fears are not well-founded.

- ▶ Determine if you currently have a commitment that's not helping you build your practice. Consider resigning from it—and do it.

CHAPTER SEVEN

Create A System For Your Marketing Activities

One of the best ways to make the most of your limited business development time is to put your marketing, as much as possible, on automatic pilot. Doing so requires you to develop systems so you know what you'll do in various situations without having to reinvent the wheel each time.

For example, what steps will you take after meeting a prospective client at a networking event? What will you do after you lose a pitch? These are recurring events that can benefit from having a predetermined plan of action.

What do you gain from having a marketing system in place?

- It dramatically increases the likelihood that you'll actually do what you had planned to do.

102

- It increases the effectiveness of your activities, because you've carefully thought through what would be appropriate (as opposed to winging it).

- It may allow you to enlist others—such as your assistant or an associate—to help in your marketing efforts because the necessary step-by-step activities are so clear.

BE PREPARED

You wouldn't think about going to court or a major negotiation without being adequately prepared. Yet, when faced with a business development lunch or networking event, many lawyers do just that—preparing, if at all, in the cab on the way to the meeting.

But with even a little preparation, the outcome of your meeting is much more likely to be successful. Here is a four-step process for making the most of marketing opportunities—whether it's a one-on-one lunch, a formal presentation, or a monthly networking event:

Determine your objective. Routinely, when I ask lawyers what their objective is for a particular marketing activity, they respond, "To get business." In most circumstances, this is an unrealistic goal. Unless the prospective client has called with a specific need or the relationship is already well developed, you won't get business from that meeting. Your goal is to continue developing the relationship so you get closer to being hired. More realistic and appropriate objectives might be to find out:

- Who does their current work

- Who is involved in decisions about hiring outside counsel

- What work is done in-house and what work is sent to outside counsel

- What are the most pressing legal issues facing their company
- Something about them, either personal or professional, that can be the basis for future contact

Marketing activities usually fall within one of the following categories:

- Relationship building
- Information seeking
- Referral requesting
- Asking for business

Be clear about what your marketing objective is before setting out for that meeting or event.

Do the necessary research. What can you find out in advance about the person or people with whom you're meeting or the company they work for? For example, if you are going to meet with someone one-on-one, you might try:

- Performing an online search to learn about the individual and his company
- Researching the type of cases that have been filed against the company in the last year
- Asking people in your network what they know about the person with whom you're meeting

Develop a list of questions. Your questions should help you achieve your objective. Having questions prepared in advance ensures that you will spend time focused on the prospect, not on you. Get a clear understanding of his needs. After all, you shouldn't be asking for business until you understand precisely what's on his agenda.

For example, if the goal of your meeting is to find out if there is an opportunity for you to represent her company on employment work, you might ask:

- What type of employment issues does your company have?

- How do you decide whether to handle your employment disputes in-house or send them to outside counsel?

- When you send them to outside counsel, is there a particular firm you use?

- How satisfied are you with your current firm?

- Are there employment issues that your current counsel doesn't have the expertise to handle?

Think of how you will follow up. How will you follow up after this meeting? Of course, your follow-up strategy won't be etched in stone, because you never know exactly what will happen at the meeting. But having a plan for follow-up has several benefits:

- It gets you thinking about the next steps to take. If you don't have future contact, it's unlikely that anything will come of the meeting.

- It ensures that you will discuss, during the meeting, how you envision following up. For example, if your plan is to invite the prospects you meet at a networking event to your firm's tax seminar, you would mention the seminar to them and ask if they're interested in attending. Or, if you plan to follow up by sending an article on an issue of personal interest, you would make sure to discover those interests in the course of conversation.

- It prepares you to ask permission to follow up. For example, you might say at the end of a lunch meeting, "I really enjoyed spending this time with you. Would it be ok if I call to set up another lunch in three months?" Or,

"Would you be interested in subscribing to our monthly newsletter? I think you would find it of value." Once you have his permission, you'll feel more committed and comfortable actually following up.

Rainmaking Action Steps

▶ Prepare for your next marketing activity by using the steps outlined above. Continue to do so before each marketing activity until it becomes something you automatically do before all of your marketing.

▶ Never leave a marketing meeting without having a clear sense of what will happen next.

HAVE A PLAN FOR HOW YOU WILL FOLLOW UP

The easiest way to make sure you follow up consistently is to have a plan in advance for how you will follow up. Create a plan for the common marketing situations you encounter. For example, decide how you will follow up after you successfully complete a matter for a client or meet someone at a networking event. What will you do immediately afterwards? How soon will you contact the prospect again? What will you do in that contact?

The plan doesn't need to be rigid, and you can improvise as each situation warrants. But the plan should specify the steps you intend to take and when.

Common scenarios for which you might have a follow-up plan include:

- You have successfully completed a matter for a client.
- You have had lunch with a prospective client.

- You have asked for a referral and received the name of a prospect.

- You have met someone at a networking event who might need your services.

- You have given a speech to an industry trade association.

- You have not been selected after a pitch or an RFP.

- You have met someone who might be a good referral source.

- You have met with a potential client who doesn't have a specific need but is generally interested in what you do.

What does a follow-up plan look like? Let's consider the example of having had lunch with someone interested in learning more about your practice. Your plan might look like this:

Action	Time frame
Send a thank-you note and your customized biography. (Don't take this with you initially, because it gives you something with which to follow up.)	Immediately
Send a follow-up article about something you discussed.	Ten days later
Send an invitation to a firm event.	One month later
Send an e-mail about something of interest.	Two months later
Call to check in.	Three months later
Send an article of interest.	Four months later
Invite to lunch.	Five months later
Send a personalized holiday card.	As appropriate

Here's an example of a follow-up plan for when you were not selected after a pitch or RFP:

Action	Time frame
Call to get specific feedback on your RFP submission or pitch.	One week later
Send an article of interest.	One month later
Call and ask if they would like to be subscribed to one of your e-alerts.	Two months later
Invite to lunch.	Three months later
Invite to a firm function, such as a seminar or a social event.	Six months later
Send a personalized holiday card.	As appropriate
Send an article of interest.	Eight months later

Rainmaking Action Steps

▸ Identify the most common situation in which you want to improve your follow-up.

▸ Create a follow-up plan for that situation, with specific activities and a time frame for when they will take place.

▸ Implement that plan.

▸ Evaluate how it is working.

▸ Tweak it to improve it.

▸ Develop a follow-up plan for another situation you commonly encounter.

GET THE MOST OUT OF NETWORKING EVENTS

For many lawyers, attending a networking event—whether sponsored by a local business organization or a bar association—has about as much appeal as going to the dentist. But while attending such events may never replace sitting on the beach drinking a margarita, it doesn't have to be painful.

The following are a few ideas to make it easier and more productive to attend these events:

Pick appropriate events. Decide whether or not to attend based on the likelihood that clients, prospective clients, and referral sources will be there. Will attending this event further your marketing goals? Networking events can be an efficient way to reconnect with the right people, but only if those people are likely to be there.

Set a specific, limited number of people with whom to connect. Keep in mind that quality interactions are more important than quantity when you set that target number. Three or four contacts may be enough, and a modest goal will make the experience much less daunting. Give yourself permission to leave once you have accomplished your goal. You might decide to reconnect with three former clients, meet two in-house counsel, or conduct informal market research by asking three attendees about their current business challenges. You're free to go once you've accomplished your objectives, but you may be surprised to discover that you're not so eager to leave once you realize it's not so difficult.

Invite someone to join you. Ask a client or prospect to attend the event with you. Even if they don't accept, it gives you a reason to contact them and stay on their radar screen. Invite someone from your firm, but only if you agree that you aren't going to hang out together.

Share your objectives for the event and find contacts for each other. Invite an outgoing associate to the event. Give him the names of the people you'd like to meet, and then set him loose.

Introduce yourself with a client-focused marketing message. When asked "What do you do?" try the following tactic. Instead of telling someone you're an environmental lawyer, which isn't likely to encourage conversation, respond with something like, "Have you seen the movie *Erin Brockovich*? Well, I represent companies faced with those kinds of problems." This response is much more likely to lead to a relationship-building conversation.

Arrive early. If you arrive just as the meal is being served or the presentation is starting, you'll miss the best time to mingle. If you're really pressed for time, show up during the reception, talk to a few people with whom you want to connect, and leave before the formal event begins.

Don't stay with people you know. Avoid hanging out with people you already know unless they are clients, potential clients, or referral sources. As one of my clients said, "If I'm talking to Dan (one of her partners), we're both wasting our time."

Prepare three topics to discuss. If there's a lull in the conversation, you'll have a topic readily at hand. Better still, think of three good questions you can ask people you meet. It will keep conversation with strangers flowing and make you feel more comfortable as you approach the event.

Get other people's cards. Conventional wisdom says to give your card to each person you meet. The conventional wisdom is wrong. When was the last time you handed out a card to someone and said something like, "If you ever need my services, please give me a call," and actually received that call? Make it your goal to get other people's cards, which gives you the opportunity to follow up. Contrary to the common adage, in this situation, *"Tis better to receive than to give."*

Follow up with those you meet. What good does it do if you spend all that time at the event connecting with people but don't stay in touch? Follow up with a nice-to-have-met-you note or e-mail, an article of interest, or an invitation to lunch.

Rainmaking Action Steps

▶ Before your next networking event, review this list of tips. Figure out which ones work for you, and use them.

▶ Keep doing that until it becomes second nature to you.

MAKE CONFERENCES WORK FOR YOU

Attending a conference or a multi-day CLE program requires a huge investment of your time. Regardless of whether you are a presenter or an attendee, make the most of that time by following these steps.

Before the event:

Decide whether it makes sense to attend. As with networking events, ask what opportunities for making good connections with clients, potential clients, and referral sources will the conference present?

Find out who might be attending. If possible, get the attendees list in advance. If your potential clients or referral sources plan to be there, set up specific times to get together—over coffee, at a meal, or during an event. Even if they're not going, checking in about the conference still provides a good opportunity to connect. Ask people you know who plan to attend, "Will there be someone at the conference you think I should meet?" If so, ask for an introduction.

Organize a dinner, breakfast, lunch, or after-dinner drinks. Invite a number of people you know or would like to know. They'll enjoy getting to meet each other and you, and you'll receive kudos as the organizer.

Take advantage of travel. If the conference is in a city other than your hometown, use it as an opportunity to reconnect with clients, colleagues, and referral sources. Tap into your contact management system to identify the people you know in the city where the conference is being held. Invite them to a have a meal or a drink with you. Even if they can't attend the event, you benefit because you've taken the time to reconnect with them.

During the event:

Follow the tips for networking events earlier in this chapter.

Organize an event on the spot. If you haven't arranged to get together with people before the conference, organize a group to have dinner or drinks together while at the conference.

Take advantage of breaks. Use this time to connect with other attendees, not to check your BlackBerry.

After the event:

Update your database with contact information on the people you met at the conference. Include a notation about how you met them, their interests, and other pertinent data.

Continue to follow up with people you met. Focus on those who seem like high-potential opportunities.

> **Rainmaking Action Step**
> ▶ Make it a habit to follow these steps before, during, and after every conference you attend.

ENSURE THAT SPEAKING ENGAGEMENTS PAY OFF

Speaking is one of the most common—and most time-consuming—marketing activity for many lawyers. To exacerbate the situation, many of my clients report that it's not particularly effective for getting new business, especially when compared to other marketing initiatives, such as face-to-face meetings with potential clients.

But if you're going to speak—and most lawyers do at some point—develop a system to make the most of the time you invest. Incorporate as many relationship-building activities as possible, and keep your eyes open for opportunities to recycle your work product.

The following are some suggestions to help you make the most of your speaking opportunities.

Before the speech:

Choose your audience carefully. Speak only to audiences that include clients, potential clients, or potential referral sources. Too often, lawyers speak to audiences of other lawyers, doing little more than educating their competition.

Speak on a topic that you want to market. An excellent land-use lawyer I know was also a partner who worked a part-time schedule. She was frequently asked to speak about how she was able to manage her schedule. However, speaking on this topic wasn't helping her grow her practice. She wanted to develop a reputation as a sophisticated land-use lawyer, not a part-time partner.

Suggest the topic on which you want to speak. If the topic proposed to you will do little to help you build your practice, suggest another. Often, organizers are more than happy to agree to your alternative.

Speak on a topic that the audience finds compelling. Of course, you want to speak about something that will enhance your reputation in a particular area, but beware of selecting a subject that is of interest mainly to you. Make sure to pick a topic that your audience wants to hear about. To figure out what this is, ask your clients and potential clients what issues concern them. Not only will it focus your presentation on a topic of interest, it will give you a great opportunity to begin a relationship with someone you'd like to know, or to strengthen a relationship with someone you haven't talked to in a while.

Invite clients, referral sources, and potential clients. Even if they can't come, at least they'll learn that you're viewed as an expert in the area.

Notify the industry press. If you can attract reporters to cover your speech, you will increase its impact and gain exposure beyond the immediate audience.

Turn it into a face-to-face marketing event. If you're moderating a panel, organize a breakfast or lunch for fellow panelists before the presentation. Or organize a faculty dinner after your speech, inviting other speakers to attend and get to know each other.

During the speech:

Be available—before and after. Don't parachute in. Often, busy lawyers arrive just before their presentation is scheduled and leave immediately after it. The most valuable aspect of your presentation is connecting with the audience before and after, so maximize that time. Wearing your speaker's badge gives you an easy opening to interact with those you meet, and it helps people feel comfortable approaching you and asking questions.

Customize your introduction. What do you want the audience to know about you? Too often, lawyers simply hand their Web site bio to the person introducing them. Because it's usually too long and detailed, the audience is lost after the third sentence. Instead, make it brief—no more than five sentences—and highlight exactly what you want this audience to know about you. If you are speaking about medical device product liability issues, your general commercial litigation experience is not relevant.

Create a way to follow up. Don't feel that you have to give away all your handouts as part of the session materials. Create a "holdback"—such as an outline, checklist, or article—to give to people who are particularly interested in your topic. Offer to send it to anyone who gives you a card at the end of your presentation.

After the speech:

Stick around to meet with attendees. You're a star—bask in it!

Send your "holdback" handout to those who requested it.

Send handouts to those who might be interested in the presentation but were not able to attend. Doing this creates another opportunity to stay in touch.

Follow up with the limited number of people you think represent the most likely prospects for you. This is probably no more than five people.

Recycle your speech. Can you turn it into an article or checklist? Can you find other opportunities to present it before a different audience?

Rainmaking Action Step

▶ At your next—and every—speaking opportunity, follow these steps before, during, and after your presentation.

TURN ARTICLE-WRITING INTO MARKETING OPPORTUNITIES

Writing articles is another time-consuming activity in which many lawyers engage. Nevertheless, most of my clients have found limited payoff from articles they have written. If you're going to write articles, keep the following in mind:

Write for your target market. Are you writing in a publication that is likely to reach current or potential clients or referral sources? Business journals and trade publications are generally much better marketing venues than legal newspapers or bar journals. If you aren't sure what publications your target market reads, ask them.

Write on topics of interest to your audience. As with speaking, lawyers too often write about matters that they find interesting, but which are too "lawyerly" or narrow to appeal to most of their clients and prospects. A great approach to ensure that your topic is relevant to your audience is to ask clients and potential clients what issues concern them most.

Write about what you want to market. Following the same strategy as you would for speaking, ask yourself if you are writing on a topic for which you want to be known. Drafting an article about interviewing witnesses when you want to be known as a construction defect litigation specialist doesn't make sense.

Solicit feedback. Consider sending your article to several people for their comments before publication. Again, it's a great opportunity to stay in touch with someone and educate them about what you do. People like to feel that you value their input.

Send the article directly to those you want to see it. Don't assume that the people you would like to read your article will actually see it when it's published. Send it to them with a note explaining why you think it will interest them.

Include contact information. Include your name, address, e-mail, phone number, and firm Web site. If you're going to all the trouble of writing something, make it easy for people to contact you if they have questions or want to hire you.

Consider self-publishing. Convert your article into a white paper, which you can send to your target list. This approach will save you the hassle and delay of dealing with decision-makers at a publication, and may reap you almost as many benefits in the eyes of your audience.

Repurpose it. Where else can it be published? Are there online opportunities? Could it be modified to make it relevant to another audience? Can it appear on your firm's Web site or be distributed as part of seminar materials?

ALWAYS HAVE AN INTERESTING ANSWER TO "WHAT'S NEW?"

How often do you get asked the question "What's new?" Certainly at least a dozen times during the average week. Lawyers have a tendency to answer the question with one of two stock responses: "Nothing much" or "I'm swamped."

Consider taking a different tack. Instead of perceiving the question as idle conversation, think of it as a chance to promote your practice. Regard it as an invitation to highlight a recent success or a certain aspect of your practice, without sounding overtly self-promoting. By providing a well-considered, yet brief, response, you can have a conversation about your work that will build both your relationship and your business.

Productive responses to "What's new?" might go something like this:

- I'm working on an interesting piece of litigation involving new nursing home regulations.

- I'm looking forward to lunch to celebrate the closing of the Shelter Island deal. You may have read about it in today's paper.

Alternatively, your response can be designed to enhance your personal relationship. Sharing an appropriate bit of personal information helps the person get to know you better. For example, you might share the following information:

- I'm still recovering from skiing over the weekend after not having done it for years.
- I'm ready to get down to work after a relaxing trip to Cancun last week.

You may discover you have something in common that will strengthen your relationship.

> One lawyer's recent experience highlights the importance of having an appropriate response to "What's new?" When her client called and posed that question, she told him that, even though she was busy, she always welcomed hearing from him because his matters were so interesting. The caller responded, "I'm glad to hear that. I have a small matter I'd like to send to you, but I hesitated because I know how busy you are." Imagine how this conversation would have unfolded if the lawyer's response had been her usual "I'm under water."

Rainmaking Action Step

▶ At the beginning of each week, decide how you'll answer the inevitable "What's new?" It can focus on a personal or professional topic.

TAKE ADVANTAGE OF MAGIC MARKETING MOMENTS

Lawyers are often so immersed in their day-to-day client work that they fail to recognize and capitalize on Magic Marketing Moments. These are the times when a client is most likely to be willing to help you in your marketing.

> I had a client apologize for not having made more progress with her marketing since our last coaching session. "I've been consumed with closing a big deal for a client," she explained. She didn't realize that she was in the middle of a Magic Marketing Moment.
>
> Because her client was delighted with her services, this was the perfect time for the lawyer to request help in her marketing efforts. She could have asked to be introduced to other lawyers in her client's legal department, or she could have requested that her client serve as a reference in the future. Given the gratitude her client was feeling, it is unlikely that she would have been turned down.

What types of situations lead to Magic Marketing Moments? Consider these:

You've obtained a successful result for a client. Every time you do an outstanding job—such as settling a case on advantageous terms or bringing in a matter under budget—you're on the cusp of a great marketing opportunity.

You've done someone a favor. Every time you do someone a favor—whether it's agreeing to speak at a conference she is organizing or recommending an overnight nanny so she can take that long-anticipated weekend away—a Magic Marketing Moment presents itself.

You weren't hired. Surprised to see that not being hired is a Magic Marketing Moment? Instead of walking away crestfallen and embarrassed when you aren't hired, increase your marketing efforts. In all likelihood, your prospective client feels slightly guilty for not hiring you. Why not help her assuage her guilt by asking her to do you a favor, such as introducing you to one of her colleagues? At the very least, it's an excellent opportunity to get feedback on why you weren't hired so you can use that learning in future pitches.

By keeping your eyes open for Magic Marketing Moments, you'll be able to increase your effectiveness. You'll still do the same great job for clients, but now you'll get support for your marketing at the same time.

Rainmaking Action Steps

▶ Write down on an index card the three Magic Marketing Moments described here. Put the card in your desk drawer where you'll see it.

▶ Once such a moment occurs, do the following:

> ▶ **Take immediate action.** The half-life of a Magic Marketing Moment is extremely short. You want to make sure your request comes while goodwill is at its peak.

> ▶ **Ask for what you want.** If your client or prospect is not in a position to send you new business, think about what else he could do to help your marketing efforts. Could he introduce you to someone you want to meet or refer you to one of his colleagues? The possibilities are limitless.

> ▶ **Follow up.** You've heard this message before. It's important. If people have promised to do something for you, ask permission to check in with them to make sure it happens.

STOCK YOUR MARKETING TOOLBOX

Every lawyer should have these tools in her marketing toolbox:

A business development plan. Know on whom you're focusing your marketing efforts and what your high-payoff activities are (see Chapters 1 and 2). Your plan should be based on a clear vision of where you want to take your practice. It should include a specific description of those to whom you're directing your marketing efforts and the particular steps you will take to market to them.

A modular bio. This enables you to customize your bio to focus your expertise on the needs of the client. For example, if you handle complex commercial litigation—including intellectual property litigation—and your client is considering you for an IP matter, you want to be able to quickly and effortlessly produce a bio that emphasizes your IP experience. Be proactive. Create a series of paragraphs describing your expertise and experience for a variety of possible representations in advance of a specific request. Then cut and paste these paragraphs as needed—whether for an introduction at a speech, to be included with a formal RFP, or for a quick e-mail to one of your colleagues who's looking to refer you.

Additional marketing materials. These should include your client list, names of people willing to serve as references, and articles you have written or which are about you. This makes it easy to give a prospect information about your services without scurrying around to collect it at the last minute.

A contact management system. It can be electronic-based (like ACT! or InterAct) or an index card system. It should allow you to capture:

- Name
- Address

- E-mail
- Telephone
- Most recent contact
- Relevant personal data (e.g., birthdays, children's names, school affiliations, etc.)
- Professional or personal interests, such as an interest in media law or cycling

Your contact management system should allow you to sort people by various categories such as geography or interests. That way, when you want to contact all your law school classmates to see who's attending your upcoming reunion, you can. Or if you find an interesting article about classic movies, you can send it to all your contacts who are classic movie buffs.

Personalized note cards. Have a supply handy so it's easy to jot down short personal messages when forwarding an article or sending a congratulatory note. People are touched to get a handwritten note in today's world of ubiquitous e-mails.

A file to capture your successes. Include client thank-you notes, as well as practice or marketing successes. These can become the basis of a bragging speech or simply serve as a way to lift your confidence when it lags.

A list of client gifts and how to order them. Use it for specific situations, such as thanking someone for a referral or celebrating milestones like having a baby or getting married.

Rainmaking Action Steps

▶ Identify one element missing from your current marketing toolbox, and commit to developing it in the next month.

▶ Add an element each month until your marketing toolbox is complete.

CHAPTER EIGHT

Forge Marketing Partnerships

Maintaining focus and momentum in marketing is a challenge for most lawyers, and client matters have a way of taking precedence over your marketing to-do list. Sometimes this is inevitable, but if it happens on a regular basis, it's time to get support to keep your marketing consistent. Create an accountability system that can help you move business development to the top of your to-do list.

HIRE A PROFESSIONAL COACH

Most people tend to honor the commitments they make to other people more than they honor the ones they make to themselves. Rather than fighting this propensity, use it to your advantage. Enlist a coach to keep you on track with your marketing, help you make the most of your time, and maintain your momentum. With the aid of a coach, you can:

- Develop a marketing approach based on your strengths
- Prepare a specific, realistic business development plan
- Focus your marketing efforts on high-potential opportunities
- Identify marketing activities that are both efficient and effective
- Prepare for specific marketing opportunities
- Become more comfortable asking for business and referrals
- Address challenges presented by specific marketing situations
- Brainstorm approaches for overcoming marketing obstacles

Making the financial investment in hiring a coach may even increase your commitment to marketing.

> **Rainmaking Action Step**
> ▶ Get support to keep you on track by hiring a coach. Nothing ensures results from your marketing efforts like consistent activity.

TEAM UP WITH A MARKETING BUDDY

If you are not willing to make the financial commitment necessary to hire a marketing coach, there is an alternative: find a marketing buddy.

The job description for your marketing buddy is someone who is as interested as you are in keeping marketing momentum going. Choose someone who would benefit from being held accountable, just as you will. Some people intentionally select a buddy who is further evolved as a marketer. It's like a runner picking a running partner who is faster than she is; it raises the bar for her performance.

Your marketing buddy can be another lawyer in your firm or one from another firm. He or she could be a professional service provider, such as an accountant, an environmental consultant, or a financial planner. Those who are not lawyers can make especially good marketing buddies, because their perspectives may be more client-like and they may have more marketing savvy than you do.

You and your buddy should meet on a regular basis—either in person or on the phone—no less than once a month. Once every two weeks would be ideal—it's long enough to give you time to get something done, but frequent enough to keep you on track. Treat your commitment to meet regularly seriously, like a client meeting or a court date. You'll benefit from the momentum you'll create.

In your meetings, talk about what you've accomplished since you last met, celebrate your successes, discuss the obstacles you may have run into, brainstorm your next steps, and most important, commit to what you will do before your next meeting.

Rainmaking Action Steps

▶ Enlist someone to be your marketing buddy.

▶ Meet regularly to keep the momentum going.

SEEK HELP FROM OTHERS IN YOUR FIRM

Your firm is home to many resources that can help you be more effective in your business development efforts. The marketing department, the librarian, your associates and assistants, and even your partners can support you in your marketing efforts. For example:

- Your assistant can help you set up a robust contact management system that will allow you to quickly and efficiently target various groups of people to whom you are marketing. You can create categories that are relevant to your business development efforts, such as women in-house counsel, people interested in biotech, and college classmates. She can do research to find and send the perfect thank-you gift for referrals. She can serve as a human tickler system to remind you to follow up with a prospect.

- The people in your marketing department can help you identify trade associations to which members of your target market belong. They can help you draft a more targeted bio or create a modular bio that you can use to target clients based on their interests. They can also help you identify cross-selling opportunities by tapping into the firm's database of top clients.

- The librarian can compile online research about a company you're targeting or about the new general counsel at an existing client. She can review case filings against a prospective client, so you can get a sense of the type of litigation in which they are involved and who has represented them in the past. She can be on the lookout for articles about existing clients, so you can stay current on the client's business and send comments on articles about the company that appear in the press.

- Your associates can review news clippings on a particular topic and highlight those worth sending along to a prospective client. They can do a first draft of an article that you can co-author for an industry publication. They can do legal research to serve as the basis for an in-house seminar for clients.

- Your partners can serve as marketing buddies. They can help you brainstorm how to approach a potential client, or be part of a team effort to market to a particular client.

To enlist the help of others, start by writing down what marketing activity you want to engage in. For example, do you want to have lunch with a prospective client, read the banking industry trade press, or participate in Leadership Chicago? Then figure out the subtasks needed to accomplish this goal. Make your list as detailed as possible. For example, to have lunch with a prospective client, you'll need to find out her e-mail address, schedule the lunch, choose a restaurant, make a reservation, and confirm it the day before. Your assistant can help you with all of these tasks.

Try to ask for help with a task that specifically draws on each individual's strengths. Your assistant might be organized and technically savvy, making the contact management project perfect for her. Your associate might have a flair for writing, so letting him tackle the first draft of an article for the industry publication would be a natural.

When asking for help on your marketing projects, convey the big picture of what you want to accomplish. For example, you might say to an associate, "I'm targeting decision-makers at Granite Rock Development Company to get their land-use business in the Sacramento area. I want to send them articles about actions of local governmental entities. Would you be willing to read the local papers to identify articles that might be appropriate?" Finally, keep those who are helping you motivated by regularly letting them know how their contributions are generating results.

Rainmaking Action Steps

▶ Enlist at least one person within your firm to help you with marketing.

▶ Identify at least three tasks on your marketing to-do list that can be delegated to that person, either in whole or in part.

CHAPTER NINE

SOME FINAL THOUGHTS

Marketing works. I can assure you of that. But it doesn't always work exactly the way you had planned. What's more, it almost never works on the timetable you would like. In spite of these obstacles, it's essential to have faith that marketing truly is effective, and keep up your effort—even when the payoff is not as immediate as you might like. Think of marketing as a marathon, rather than a sprint.

When it comes to marketing, patience is definitely a virtue. So is the ability to refrain from taking rejection personally. Only with this perspective can your marketing have the consistency that it needs to work.

BE PATIENT

I have some good news and some bad news for you, and the news is the same: business development takes time.

The good news is that you don't have to feel like a failure if you don't get business from every lunch or networking event you attend. The bad news is that you aren't likely to get business from attending only one lunch or networking event.

It typically takes seven to nine significant contacts before you can convert a prospect into a client. It would not be unusual for it to take 18 months of consistent marketing to land a client.

Not all worthwhile marketing activities produce immediate results. Some lead to referral sources, some bring about increased visibility among prospective clients, some deepen a relationship with an existing client. Any of these may lay the groundwork for future business. But know that small, consistent marketing actions get results.

Of course, this is not to say that you should continue to market to a prospect regardless of the feedback you are receiving or the results you are seeing. Patience is a virtue—to a point. But there may come a time when you have to conclude that a particular prospect is just not likely to turn into business. I wish I had a magic formula to tell you when that moment has arrived. But as long as your marketing is focused and your activities are appropriate, the need to throw in the towel should be infrequent.

Rainmaking Action Step

▶ Market consistently. Be persistent. Trust that you will see results. You will.

DON'T TAKE REJECTION PERSONALLY

Nobody likes being rejected. But the fact is, not all of your marketing efforts will pay off. When rejection occurs—whether it's losing a pitch for a new piece of business or when someone doesn't return your phone call—you have a choice. You can either be paralyzed by your lack of success or you can bounce back and try again. Which option you pick is a matter of mindset.

Consider adopting one of the following mindsets the next time you are feeling self-doubt:

- Separate yourself from your services. Someone can still like you, trust you, and respect you, but not have a need for your services.

- People can hire you only when they have a need for the services you're providing. They may not need your services right now, or someone else might already be meeting that need. That's unfortunate, but it does not reflect poorly on you or your services.

- What you have to offer may not be a match for their needs. Perhaps they need someone with more geographic reach than your firm provides. Perhaps their management has a need to use a firm with a brand name.

- People are busy. Returning your phone calls or responding to your e-mails may not be as high a priority for them as it is for you.

- Some sales take a long time. You're building a relationship that will ultimately result in long-term business (if you just stay the course).

- Your expectations about the likely result of your marketing activities may be unrealistic. It is extremely rare for someone to be hired after just one lunch.

Rainmaking Action Steps

▶ De-personalize your reaction to any less-than-successful marketing forays.

▶ Don't let small rejections get in the way of maintaining your marketing momentum.

Conclusion

In concluding this book, I've chosen to share a personal story about how I got "into action." My hope is that the lessons I've learned will help you, as well.

Business development comes naturally to me—exercising on a regular basis does not. Why is that relevant to this book? It turns out that I have learned a lot about how to get started and stay motivated with business development by reflecting on how I was finally able to maintain an exercise regime.

Although I know that exercising is good for me, that knowledge wasn't enough to get me moving. Only after I had a serious health scare did I realize how important my physical well-being truly is. Regular exercise became part of my prescription for ongoing health, and it's now as much a part of my regimen as eating and sleeping.

With this analogy in mind, the following are a few tips to make business development a regular part of your work week:

Get clear on why you're building your practice. Just as I figured out why maintaining my health is important to me, you need to figure out why having your own book of business is important to you—not in the general sense, but in the personal, specific sense. (If you are having trouble articulating this, refer back to Chapter 6.)

Realize that getting started is the hardest part. I had lots of excuses for not exercising. It was too hot. I was too tired. I had to get to the office to finish a project. Similarly, you can come up with lots of reasons for not marketing. You are buried under client work. You aren't good at it. You work with a partner who feeds you a steady stream of work. Women just aren't good at promoting themselves.

But these rationalizations are getting in the way of the activity you need to do to have a satisfying, lucrative practice. Once you take that first step, the most difficult part is behind you.

Start out with baby steps. I asked my personal trainer what my target heart rate should be. She replied, "Let's get you exercising five times a week for thirty minutes each time. Then we can start worrying about whether you're in your target heart-rate zone. The important thing is making this a habit."

Funny I had missed that, since it mirrors my advice to my own clients.

Yes, I believe you should engage in business development on a daily basis and be in touch with your hottest prospects monthly—but first, get in the habit of working consistently on business development. If that means doing it three days a week and contacting your hottest prospects only once a quarter, so be it (for starters).

Let go of "shoulds" and do what works. Over the past ten years, I've worked with several personal trainers. Once I got the routine down, I felt like I "should" be able to do it on my own. Guess what happened when I stopped working with a trainer? Within weeks, I quit working out altogether.

I've been through this cycle about five times (apparently, I'm a slow learner), and have finally accepted that if I'm going to work out regularly, I need a trainer's support. Since my health is important to me, I'm willing to do what it takes—in this case, spend the money and hire a trainer—for that to happen.

By the same token, it's essential to stop worrying about how you "should" approach business development and start focusing on what it will take to get it done. Perhaps, like me, you need a coach to hold you accountable. Maybe it's time to give up on those half-finished articles and replace them with something that's productive and enjoyable— like having lunch with an existing client. Perhaps you can make a deal with yourself that you'll attend one networking event a month—and give yourself permission to leave after 30 minutes.

Determine what it takes for you to be involved in business development on a consistent basis and then do it—without worrying about how you think it should be done.

Just do it. For weeks, I struggled to create the perfect schedule. Should I take Tuesday or Wednesday off? Should I work out Monday and Thursday mornings and Tuesday and Friday nights? Should Monday's cardio be walking or elliptical training? (You think I'm kidding? I'm not.)

Finally, my trainer said, "Set your alarm tomorrow morning and just do it." It was the kick I needed. Is my current schedule perfect? No. Do I occasionally miss days? Yes. But I am exercising on a regular basis, which is a lot more than I did in the past.

When approaching business development, lawyers often spend too much time trying to figure things out instead of taking action. Instead, you have to *just do it*. Don't let the perfect get in the way of the good. Call the client you've been meaning to reconnect with today, even if you don't have the ideal opener for the conversation. Schedule lunch with that past referral source to ask for another referral, even if it's been a year since you last spoke. Walk down the hall and talk to your partner about that cross-selling opportunity, even if you're not sure about how it will be received.

When you do these things, you'll be exercising your marketing muscles. And with that newfound strength, you'll be well on your way to getting the results you want.

Resources

The books listed below will provide additional support for your rainmaking activities.

FOCUSING YOUR EFFORTS

Focus: The Future of Your Company Depends on It
Al Ries
Harper Business Essentials, 2005

This book advocates that focus is a key ingredient to generate effective marketing and a successful practice. To ensure that you stand for something in your clients' or prospects' minds, the author states that you must narrow the focus of your services and marketing. Without it, you confuse your clients, squander marketing resources, and ultimately produce less desirable results. Although all the examples cited in the book are drawn from the business world, the points made apply equally to the legal market.

Niche and Grow Rich
Jennifer Basye Sander and Peter Sander
Entrepreneur Press, 2003

While this book is not specifically written for the legal market (and much of it will be of little interest to lawyers), read "Six Steps to Evaluating a Niche." The information provided will serve as a key resource to help you define and evaluate a potential niche for your practice.

IDENTIFYING YOUR STRENGTHS

Soar with Your Strengths
Donald O. Clifton and Paula Nelson
Dell, 1996

This book articulates one of the central themes of ClientFocus' work: concentrate on your strengths and manage around your weaknesses. Rather than trying to fix your weak points, Clifton and Nelson argue that you should leverage your strong ones. The authors help you identify your strengths while providing strategies to deal with your weaknesses.

Now, Discover Your Strengths
Marcus Buckingham and Donald O. Clifton
Free Press, 2001

In keeping with the basic premise of *Soar with Your Strengths*, this book reinforces the concept that high achievement stems from exercising your strengths, not trying to improve your weaknesses. Based on extensive research, it provides a detailed examination of how to identify and build on your strengths. Additionally, it includes an online assessment tool to help you identify your top five strong points.

StrengthsFinder 2.0
Tom Rath
Gallup Press, 2007

This book features the latest version of the online assessment tool developed by the Gallup Organization (which initially appeared in *Now, Discover Your Strengths*) and offers an abbreviated explanation of the various strengths it identifies.

CREATING A BUSINESS DEVELOPMENT PLAN

Creating Your Future: Personal Strategic Planning for Professionals
George L. Morrisey
Berrett-Koehler Publishers, 1992

Rich with useful exercises to help develop a personal and professional vision, this book guides you toward identifying specific steps to achieve that vision. Written for professional service providers, the language and examples resonate with lawyers' experiences.

SETTING GOALS

The Magic Lamp: Goal Setting for People Who Hate Setting Goals
Keith Ellis
Three Rivers Press, 1998

In spite of the title, if you truly hate goal setting, you might want to leave this book on the shelf. However, if you're in the market for guidance to help establish and achieve professional goals, this book offers solid techniques and motivation.

BUSINESS DEVELOPMENT STRATEGIES AND TACTICS

Business Development for Lawyers: Strategies for Getting and Keeping Clients
Sally J. Schmidt
ALM Publishing, 2006

Written specifically for lawyers, this book offers a variety of ways to develop business and appropriately distinguishes the relative efficacy of these various tactics. As any good marketing book should, it encourages client focus and emphasizes the development of strong personal relationships. It also highlights the importance of preparation and follow-up in all situations, from attendance at a conference to lunch with a client.

Book Yourself Solid: The Fastest, Easiest, and Most Reliable System for Getting More Clients Than You Can Handle Even if You Hate Marketing and Selling
Michael Port
John Wiley & Sons, 2006

This book provides practical advice about the strategies that service professionals (yes, that includes lawyers) can use to grow their businesses. He advises selecting strategies that draw on your strengths. While the book's New Age flavor may be off-putting to some readers, its central themes of identifying your ideal clients, discovering their needs, and selling to those needs provide solid advice for even the most conservative lawyer. Its exercises will help you identify effective, comfortable ways to promote yourself.

Managing the Professional Service Firm
David H. Maister
Free Press, 2004

A former Harvard Business School professor, the author works with major law, accounting, and consulting firms. In this book, he offers intelligent, clear, and practical advice. While the content focuses on law firm management issues, gems abound for the individual, as well. Of particular interest are the chapters on "The Business Development Package," "Marketing to Existing Clients," and "The Under Delegation Problem."

Get Clients NOW! A 28-Day Marketing Program for Professionals, Consultants and Coaches!
C.J. Hayden
American Management Association, 2006

While a 28-day system for getting more clients may not be a realistic time frame for the complex marketing and sales process of a typical legal matter, this book offers an intelligent and strategic approach to the process of marketing.

CREATING BALANCE IN YOUR LIFE

Work Less, Make More: Stop Working So Hard and Create the Life You Really Want!
Jennifer White
John Wiley & Sons, 1999

This book outlines ten steps that enable you to spend less time working while still reaping the benefits of increased income and an enjoyable, fulfilling lifestyle. Chapters on "Do What You Do Best" and "The Power of Focus" are particularly relevant and important.

Coming Up for Air: How to Build A Balanced Life in A Workaholic World
Beth Sawi
Hyperion, 2000

Written by a former executive vice president of Charles Schwab & Co., this book advises how to lead a balanced life while faced with a demanding career. The author encourages readers to identify "personal priorities," examine motivations for working hard, and recognize "the relative value" of an extra hour of work versus an hour devoted to other tasks. Practical approaches for a priority-based life abound, including managing technology, using your commute productively, developing strategies for especially busy times, and saying no.

Turn It Off: How to Unplug from the Anytime-Anywhere Office Without Disconnecting Your Career
Gil Gordon
Three Rivers Press, 2001

Technology tools such as e-mails, BlackBerrys, and voice mail have made it possible to work seamlessly wherever you are. However, this accessibility has blurred the lines between work and personal time. This book offers exercises to help gauge the impact that the use of technology is having on your life. It encourages you to realize that you have choices in deciding when to "shut the office door." Many of its observations are equally applicable to creating boundaries between work and personal time.

OVERCOMING FEAR OF SELF-PROMOTION

Brag! The Art of Tooting Your Own Horn Without Blowing It
Peggy Klaus
Business Plus, 2004

To overcome the fear of self-promotion, the author encourages you to talk about yourself and your accomplishments with "authenticity, pride, and enthusiasm." Using sample conversations, self-evaluation surveys, advice on avoiding common bragging pitfalls, and other concrete tips, Klaus guides readers in the fine art of bragging. Chapter 2 poses ten questions, the answers to which will help you develop your "bragologue." Chapter 6, "Performance Reviews," will help you put your best self forward when it comes to writing your compensation memo.

RELATIONSHIP BUILDING

Vital Friends: The People You Can't Afford to Live Without
Tom Rath
Gallup Press, 2006

The author believes that the quality of the relationships you have with the people with whom you work dramatically affects your satisfaction and productivity at work. It may sound like fluff, but it isn't. The book, produced by the Gallup Organization, is supported by extensive research. What it says about friendships in the workplace applies equally to relationships with clients, potential clients, and referral sources. After all, people like to do business with people they like. The book makes specific suggestions for strengthening relationships based on the role you fill in the other person's life.

Nonstop Networking: How to Improve Your Life, Luck, and Career
Andrea Nierenberg
Capital Books, 2002

Most books about networking are, as one client said, "goofy." This short book is a refreshing exception. Providing a systematic approach to networking that focuses on building long-term relationships, the author offers advice on follow-up and creating a system to track contacts. The chapter on "Networking for Introverts" provides tactics for those who find networking events uncomfortable.

She Wins, You Win: The Most Important Rule Every Businesswoman Needs to Know
Gail Evans
Gotham, 2004

The author's frankly feminist book argues that women need to create and support women's networks. Her premise is, "Any time any woman succeeds in business, your chances of succeeding in business increase, and any time any woman fails in business, your chances of failing increase." While you may not agree with all of her recommendations ("Always try to send business to a woman" and "Never speak ill of other women"), it encourages creative thinking about how to get business by using a women's network. Each chapter ends with specific action steps that serve as good reminders of how to make the most of your network.

SELLING

The Woman Lawyer's Rainmaking Game: How to Build a Successful Law Practice
Silvia L. Coulter
Thomson LegalWorks, 2004

Not for women lawyers only, this book is a good primer on how to sell legal services. It emphasizes the importance of discovering what clients want, the need for following up and staying in touch, and the skills required for building strong relationships.

WOMEN IN LAW FIRMS

Ending the Gauntlet: Removing Barriers to Women's Success in the Law
Lauren Stiller Rikleen
Thomson LegalWorks, 2006

Although this is not a business development book, it is well worth your time if you are concerned about promoting and retaining women lawyers in law firms. Unlike many authors who address the issue of women's slow progress in law firms, Rikleen focuses on the structure of the firms themselves as the real culprit in women's exodus from law firms and their failure to join the partnership ranks. In her meticulously researched book, the author points to institutional impediments in recruitment, retention, and advancement of women.

About the Author

Sara Holtz coaches successful women lawyers to become successful rainmakers.

Since moving from an in-house legal career to founding ClientFocus in 1995, she has worked with hundreds of women lawyers from the nation's leading firms to help them grow their practices. Before 1995, Holtz practiced law in-house for 13 years, serving as Vice President and General Counsel of Nestlé Beverage Company and Division Counsel for the Clorox Company. She was the first woman chair of the Association of Corporate Counsel, the world's leading professional organization for in-house counsel.

Holtz has been a featured expert in articles in the *American Lawyer*, *ABA Journal*, *USA Today*, *Los Angeles Daily Journal*, *San Francisco Daily Journal*, *California Lawyer*, *Perspectives* (the publication of the ABA Commission on Women), *Harvard Law School Bulletin*, and other professional journals. Articles she has written have appeared in the *American Lawyer*, *House Counsel*, *San Francisco Daily Journal*, and *New Jersey Lawyer*. Her presentations have included numerous

ABA programs, including The Presidential Showcase at the ABA's Annual Meeting, as well as presentations for the National Association of Women Lawyers, Legal Marketing Association, California Women Lawyers, Harvard Law School, and the State Bar of New York.

The State Bar of California has honored Holtz for "outstanding leadership of the in-house community." She was named one of "20 People to Watch" by *Sacramento Magazine* for her work with the Women Rainmakers Roundtable. She was a finalist for the *Sacramento Bee's* Athena Award, honoring women who assist other women in reaching their full potential.

Holtz graduated *magna cum laude* from Yale College and *cum laude* from Harvard Law School.

You can subscribe to her monthly newsletter, *Focus on Rainmaking,* on her Web site at www.clientfocus.net. She can be reached at holtz@clientfocus.net.